First Steps to Seeing

Praise for *First Steps to Seeing*

'Emma Kidd is a practical visionary and her book, *First Steps to Seeing* is a most useful companion on our journey of transformation. Read this book – you will be delighted.'

Satish Kumar, Editor-in-Chief,
Resurgence & Ecologist magazine

'By offering many practical exercises and personal experiences, Emma helps us to discover the missed dimension of cognition in perception, opening up a new window on the world. *First Steps to Seeing* is a deeply insightful guide for anyone wishing to fully experience a more meaningful life, and engage more authentically with people, our organisations and the environment.'

Simon Robinson, co-author of
Holonomics: Business Where People and Planet Matter

'I love Emma's book and the expression she gives to "work as the gift" – this resonates deeply with me. How we value ourselves, whether we choose to view our work as a gift and whether we self-determine our own happiness – that is our gift, should we choose to see it. Emma's wonderful book opens us up to a whole new way of seeing.'

Polly Higgins, CEO, Earth Community Trust, and author of
Eradicating Ecocide, Earth is our Business and
I Dare You to Be Great

First Steps *to* Seeing

A Path Towards Living Attentively

Emma Kidd

Floris Books

Published in 2015 by Floris Books
© 2015 Emma Kidd

 This book is also available
as an eBook

British Library CIP Data available
ISBN 978-178250-169-5
Printed in Great Britain by Page Bros Ltd.

Contents

In loving memory of Kirsten Llewellyn

1976–2015

Whose smile was brighter than a sky full of stars.

Acknowledgments

First Steps to Seeing was only able to come-into-being by temporarily 'stepping out' of my everyday life. This would not have been possible without the unconditional love and support of my friends and family along the way, to all of whom I am extremely grateful. I would particularly like to thank my parents for putting a roof over my head and accepting my rather 'radical' choices in life with love and without question. This applies also to friends such as Alex, Ben and Zemfira, Clara and the Ashburton 'crew', Robert Woodford, Tilley and Mirella, Yannick Beaudoin, Nic and Sam, Gemma, and Carly. I would also like to thank Johan for his unwavering belief in, and enthusiasm for, my love of writing. Similarly, I am extremely grateful to Simon Robinson for encouraging me to share my thoughts and words, and for generously providing the platform upon which to do so.

Many heartfelt thanks are due to my friend and colleague Alexander Balerdi for being a dear companion to me and my nascent ideas, and not least for introducing me to a dynamic way of seeing in regards to interpersonal relationships. Alex introduced me to much of the research that I have referenced in Chapter 7.

I would like to thank Schumacher College in Devon for all the wonderful opportunities they have given me, both to learn and to teach. In particular, I would like to thank Philip Franses for his support with my thesis, and for creating the Process and Pilgrimage lectures and conferences that allowed me to continue my inquiries with Henri Bortoft long after my official studies had ended.

I am very grateful to my editor at Floris Books, Christopher Moore, for 'seeing' this book before it even existed, and then for supporting me along the way.

My deep thanks also go out to the wonderful staff at the ASHA centre in Gloucestershire, such as Adrian Locher and Mark Gifford, who gave me free reign to teach, and thus to extend, many of the ideas that are in this book. The students at ASHA lovingly demanded a new clarity and accessibility from myself and my ideas that this book has very much benefited from.

Last, but most certainly not least, I would like to thank my good friend Judy Allen for assisting me during the writing of this book. Without question Judy's love, support, time and patience have made me a better writer and helped make *First Steps to Seeing* the best it can be. Words cannot express how grateful I am to have had such a wonderful person actively participate in the coming-into-being of this book.

Emma Kidd
Norfolk, England
March 2015

Author's Preface

I have always had what you could call, a 'keen eye', and a natural attentiveness towards my sensory experience in general. I love observing and sensing life. However, despite my professional background in design, and my lifelong passion for photography, I now realise that I had not given much attention to the *process of seeing* whilst I was caught up in the everyday rush of life and work. Seeing was something I just 'did' and got paid to do – that is, until I met Henri Bortoft.

What led me to first study with Henri in 2008 at Schumacher College in Devon, England, was unfortunately not my love for seeing but my intense discomfort with what my eyes had *seen* whilst travelling and working overseas as a lingerie designer. During my years spent designing and developing garments for mass-production I got to *see* the size and scale of the fashion industry with my own eyes; and whilst visiting the factories that manufactured my designs I gained a poignant first-hand experience of the way in which the people who made these garments were treated with a distinct lack of humanity, as though they were no more than just parts of a machine.

After much time spent researching the business models and economic systems which were driving this industry, I soon understood that, at that time, I could not change this cold, mechanical approach to design, to business, and to life, from the inside. Therefore, I left the fashion industry to investigate alternative ways of thinking about and doing business. What I did not expect, when leaving my 'life' and profession behind me, is that these explorations would take me right back to the very foundation upon which my career in design had initially been built, my way of seeing.

The dynamic way of seeing that I will be describing to you within this book is *dynamic* by nature and, as such, has no set form. In some sense it is similar to a chameleon, actively seeking to make itself invisible so that it can unify, as much as is possible, with the life that it is directly experiencing. It is this chameleon-like tendency of a dynamic way of seeing that has led to some quite unlikely sources of research and case studies being referenced in this book, these include: 'self-help' books, a Welsh jeans manufacturer, a study of failing marriages, and an educational initiative for schools which does not aim to 'teach' anything. What is most important in this seemingly bizarre collection of sources is not *what* they each 'appear' to be, but the *way* in which they have each come-into-being. Consequently, as with everything we encounter in life, I would encourage you to 'notice' any judgments that arise in relation to these unusual sources but then to set those thoughts to one side in order to give these studies and projects your full attention.

Far from presenting this work as a paragon of perfection I offer it more as a record of my knowledge and experience to date, a collection of 'noticings'. It is also very much a platform upon which I can share the noticings of others, not least, the work of the late Henri Bortoft. I am eternally grateful to Henri for turning my world upside down, and for turning my way of seeing the right way up. I very much hope that this book will serve, at least in part, as a beginners' guide to Henri's work and will inspire the reader to explore his work first-hand in *The Wholeness of Nature* and *Taking Appearance Seriously*.

Therefore, as a gift of appreciation and gratitude for all that I have been blessed with in life so far – the good, the bad and the ugly – I would like to share my thoughts, insights and experiences with you in the hope that they may then set you onto your own journeys and discoveries; enabling you to fully participate in, and to co-create with, the wonder of what it means-to-be a human being, right here, right now, on this fascinating earth.

Introduction: Living Through the Senses

Before I start introducing this book, I invite you to stop for a moment. Use this opportunity to temporarily step away from the rush of everyday life, to slow down and to give full attention to your sensory experience, right here and right now. When you have finished reading this paragraph, set a timer on your watch or phone for two minutes, close your eyes and focus your complete attention on experiencing life through your senses. First, take a few deep breaths and then pay attention to the soles of your feet as they rest upon the ground. From there, slowly guide your attention up your legs until you reach your torso and observe how it feels reclining in your seat. Finally, lead your awareness up through your abdomen, chest and neck, right up to the top of your head, and focus your attention on your thoughts. Take a moment to notice what your thoughts are doing. Whether they are judging or analysing this exercise, or filling your mind with a to-do list, pay attention to them briefly, accept them and then let them go. For the remainder of the time enjoy gently sitting still, with your attention open to the world. Start your two minutes now.

To develop a practice of living attentively I invite you to repeat this short exercise every time that you pick this book up to start reading again, whether you last got through two pages or two chapters. The exercise serves as preparation, in part, for what this whole book is inviting us to do – that is to slow down and to give our full attention to noticing the life that surrounds us, both inside and outside of ourselves. This gesture of slowing down and giving our whole attention to life, one experience at a time, is what we seem least able to do in our frenetic modern lives. Therefore, in view of the countless social and global issues that appear to accompany this fractured way of life, this book brings the process of 'living attentively' to the forefront of our attention.

To get us started, the chapters of this book form a series of stepping stones that can lead us towards developing the dynamic way of seeing that is needed in order to give life our full attention. However, at the end of the day, these words are only, '... like fingers pointing at the moon, not to be mistaken for the moon itself'.[1] Each chapter is designed, not to provide knowledge, as such, but to offer an invitation for us to explore and experience the processes that it describes for ourselves.

First Steps to Seeing is designed to take us on a journey, one that encourages us to fully notice life by paying acute attention to the ways in which we see, think and act, every day. I would be deceiving you if I did not warn you that this type of inquiry is not for the faint hearted. As we move through the book we will begin noticing, and fully experiencing, aspects of life that we do not usually notice in day-to-day life. Depending on the depth of attention that we bring to this process, this 'noticing' may elicit extreme highs, and moments of intense wonder and amazement. However, the process of giving our full attention to life, as radically and as honestly as we can, is challenging, and it may well also shed light on aspects of the world that we would rather not see. Making an effort to really see ourselves as we are and to see the world *as it is* takes courage, it requires us to let go of everything that we think we already know and to open ourselves to the unexpected, whatever that may be.

In Part One there is a series of practical exercises embedded within the chapters which are designed to bring our attention to experiences, and to habits of mind, that we routinely do not notice. The exercises in Chapter 1 will demonstrate that there is 'more to seeing than meets the eye' and turn our attention towards the ways in which our minds automatically define, and organise, everything that we rest our eyes upon. The exercises in Chapter 2 then require us to set aside these perceptual and intellectual shortcuts, which we normally rely on everyday, so that we can focus our full attention on our sensory experience.

This process of intentionally bypassing our own in-built, time-saving methods of seeing the world can, at times, feel quite frustrating, as our minds love shortcuts! However, despite any initial frustration that may emerge, I encourage you to persevere. What our minds fail to show us on a moment-by-moment basis, whilst delivering these convenient ways of side-stepping life, is that just beyond these cognitive shortcuts is a sense-perceptible world which is more alive, complex and full of expression than it is possible to know until we have experienced this complexity and dynamism for ourselves.

Aside from our own habits of mind, which distract our attention away from our experience of life, with the rise of mobile technology and the ever-increasing speed of communication today we have also become intimately acquainted with digital distractions. These additional diversions, such as constant alerts pinging on our mobile devices, fracture and splinter our focus and attention. As a result, we are less and less used to the lingering immediacy of participating with only one experience at a time.

First Steps to Seeing offers an antidote to these seductive distractions by providing a pathway towards living attentively which makes it possible for us to rediscover our own experience of life. As the scientist John Medina writes in his book *Brain Rules*, 'The brain's attentional "spotlight" can focus on only one thing at a time'.[2] Therefore, our capacity to pay attention is not capable of multi-tasking. Focusing our attention on just one experience at a time seems to be the way in which our brains work and learn 'best'. This is exactly what 'living attentively' does, it involves experiencing the process of fully attending to our experience of life. That is, noticing our experience of life as we are experiencing it, rather than analysing it after the event.

In Chapters 2, 3 and 4 we will explore the way in which paying full attention to life develops our innate capacity to get to know life in terms of itself and on its own terms. This process involves extending our understanding far beyond the definitive forms of knowledge that we commonly produce in order to tell us about life. Instead of relying on pre-conceived knowledge, this way of seeing life requires us to notice the qualities, patterns and relationships through which parts of life naturally express their essential nature and unique character.

Therefore, the process of paying full attention to life, as it is laid out in this book, involves temporarily leaving all that we think we know about life behind. This means letting go of what we think we already know about our husband or wife, our boss or colleague, our clients or students, our organisation or city, and then learning to immerse ourselves in the 'other' in order to think *with* them. We will do this by refining our skills of focus and attention, and exercising our capacities to fully notice, describe, imagine, open ourselves to, and reflect upon, our lived experience as precisely as possible.

In Part Two we will explore how our way of seeing is directly connected to the way we relate to ourselves, and also to those around us. This is incredibly important for our personal lives, our relationships and for all of the interactions that we have with other people, every single day. By developing an understanding that there is more to seeing than meets the eye we can begin to open ourselves to seeing our friends, loved ones, colleagues, and even strangers, with a greater clarity; and through becoming aware that there is also more to hearing than meets our ears we can bring a greater degree of focus and attention to the way we speak with, relate to and listen to, other people.

Living attentively, in our personal and professional lives, enables us to transform the way in which we relate to ourselves, to other people, to our work and to life in general. When we practise this dynamic way of seeing, and relating, we create the possibility of seeing further, of feeling deeper, and of noticing more – in other words, becoming more fully human. We can then start to use ourselves as accurate instruments to gather a living knowledge of life *as it is* and in context. In Chapters 6, 7 and 8 we will then explore how this 'living knowledge' can inform the ways in which we live our lives, the ways we work, and the ways we design and create the systems and organisations that our lives and work are built around.

Despite the sober disclaimer which came at the beginning of this introduction, in essence this book is a practical, playful guide in how to fully encounter the livingness of life and how to learn to think in accordance with life itself. As much as possible, the inquiry can and should be undertaken with gentleness and with joy. Regardless of the challenging realisations that it might present along the way, the process of living attentively is not something that we need suffer through. Practising the sustained, focused attention and empathic openness that a dynamic way of seeing requires can offer us many experiential benefits. For us as individuals, on a day-to-day level the practice can improve our focus, attention, and concentration. It can also bring many of the associated physical, and emotional, health benefits apparent in other contemplative practices, such as mindfulness and meditation, like stress reduction, and improved well-being.

Developing a dynamic way of seeing and relating to life asks us to become more gentle, vulnerable, open and intimate in our encounters with the world. It requires us to be much more attentive to our experience than our everyday perception usually allows and to be radically more direct and disciplined in describing our experiences of life. Through doing this we can begin a process of 'leaning back' from our everyday lives, and 'business as usual', in order to honestly explore life *as it is*. This enables us to develop a fresh perspective on life, whilst still remaining connected to our own experience, and allows us to commence a journey towards wholly understanding life, *as it is*, and in terms of itself.

Part One: Developing a Dynamic Way of Seeing

1. More to Seeing than Meets the Eye ...

I can see a holly tree

When I look out of my window I can see a holly tree. At first glance this sentence appears to be pretty straightforward, it provides a simple indication of what I am *seeing*. The sentence itself is factually correct, if I look up from my desk right now I *can* see a holly tree in my garden. However, these words tell us almost nothing in relation to what I am actually seeing with my eyes, right here, right now, when I look out of my window. Let's try a different approach:

> The tree I can see is only partially visible as my view is interrupted by the straight, white edges which form the corner of my window. What is visible is a large pear-shaped, complicated mass of mottled green and yellow 'foliage' that is punctuated with small collections of radiant, bright red dots. The foliage seems to consist of many small, pointed, oval shape 'leaves' which are densely clustered together on a multitude of separate, elongated branches. These leaves have a dark green centre, similar to the colour of evergreen pines, and a thick, irregular, light-yellow coloured outer edge. Each leaf seems to have a glossy shine. The mass of foliage, as a whole, is also covered in areas of darkness and spots of bright light; there are patches of deep shade where the tree's branches block out the sun's light, and a multitude of bright white spots where the gloss of the leaves seems to reflect the light. I also notice that the tree has visitors, two small songbirds are perched on its uppermost branches.

In contrast to the initial sentence, the descriptive paragraph above comes much closer to conveying my experience of *seeing*. The first sentence tried to tell us what I was seeing but it really only succeeded in sharing an abstract idea of 'what' was being seen. Therefore, in order to express a more accurate portrayal of what I was actually seeing with my eyes (to *show* what I was seeing) I had to pay full attention to my sensory experience. This involved making an effort to notice some of the particular qualities and details of the 'holly tree' and to describe those experiences as precisely as possible.

By comparing the initial sentence with the longer paragraph we can begin to recognise the details of life which we routinely miss when we rely on our mind to define what our eyes are seeing. I used the term 'holly tree' in the initial sentence to evoke a general idea of what I was seeing. However, by doing this, I was not describing what I was actually seeing with my eyes at all. Instead, I was stating my mind's idea of what it thought I had seen. This idea, 'holly tree', jumped into my awareness as soon as my eyes rested on the actual tree – it was my mind's 'best guess' at quickly making sense of my experience. This automatic cognitive process reduced my rich, complex, sensory experience into a simple, universally recognisable form, in the blink of an eye.

This cognitive process of transforming the complex experience of seeing into a simple idea, such as 'holly tree', is similar to typing in shorthand. In a very simple yet sophisticated way it allows us to represent the life we are experiencing with the minimal amount of time and effort possible. However, in order to do this, these representations only reflect the universal nature of what *has been* seen – they do not reflect the unique nature of the life that we are seeing as-we-are-seeing it, in the present moment.

This giant leap from experience to thought usually happens every moment of the day without us even realising it. Instead of dwelling in the process of seeing long enough to notice the exact details that we are experiencing with our eyes, our attention tends to get quickly distracted by what we *think* we are seeing, such as a 'holly tree', and then diverted to what we think we know about it. On the one hand, in everyday life, this is a very necessary and useful way of processing our experience. It means that we can develop and sustain a basic understanding of what a part of life is, and does, without needing to re-discover it and learn about it afresh every time that we meet it.

Let's take a 'car' for example. Once we think we know the basics of what a car looks like and what it does – such as the fact that cars have wheels, can travel at immense speeds and can kill us if we step in front of them whilst they are moving – our attention is swiftly moved away from our direct sensory experience of the particular car that is in front of us, and redirected to the 'car' idea in our mind. This 'car' idea not only allows us to recognise cars but it also informs the ways we interact with them. As such the idea itself is like an iceberg; when we see a car in everyday life our attention is brought to the tip of the iceberg, the 'car' idea (this is our awareness of seeing what our mind recognises to be a car). However, all the general information we know about cars is attached under water, under the surface of our awareness, so that every time we define our visual sense experience as 'car' we just know what to do without having to think much about it. For example, if we want to cross a road without being killed we automatically avoid stepping in front of moving cars. Imagine how dangerous it would be if we had to learn from scratch what a car is, and does, every time we encountered one, it would prove fatal to many of us!

The wonder of our mind's ability to instantly define what we think we are seeing is exactly this, it makes it possible for us to navigate our lives safely, efficiently, and effectively every day. By using universal 'names' or 'labels' to define and recall knowledge about everything that we see we can walk across a road without getting knocked over, arrive at work on time and in one piece, and find our way home without getting lost, all without much conscious effort. By filtering out (diverting our attention away from) all of the unique details and qualities of life, which still meet our eyes, our mind greatly reduces the complexity of our surroundings. It then re-presents these complex, unique details with a set of very basic ideas that indicate *what* is in our vicinity, such as a bridge, a river, a road, a tree, or a red traffic light.

Contrary to the smooth, straightforward way in which our mind defines life, as a series of 'familiar' forms that we perceive to be the 'same', we are actually bombarded by newness every minute of every day, we just do not tend to pay attention to it. Our senses are relentlessly confronted with a constant stream of fresh, new experiences but our minds quickly organise this newness into a series of recognisable, universal ideas. The result is that we end up experiencing the familiarity of these ideas and end up disconnected from the actual diversity that our senses experience.

When our attention is drawn to these universal ideas, such as the idea of a 'car', we notice only what tends to be the 'same' in life, for example, a car tends to have a set of four wheels, an engine, a chassis, at least two seats and some windows. This focus on tendencies and sameness, stops us from being overwhelmed by the constantly changing, dynamic, diverse nature of life itself. If we did not have this ability to categorise, define and store general information about life we would live in a world of perpetual newness, our attention would constantly be at the mercy of our environment and we would continuously be pulled toward the uniqueness of every part of life that we encountered. Without this ability to quickly define life, every time that we laid our eyes on a car, a tree or a person we would see them as if for the 'first' time, over and over again. However, this way in which our minds routinely define and make sense of our visual experience also has significant drawbacks.

Once our mind has defined *what* we are experiencing, we often stop paying attention to *how* our senses are experiencing it. This redirection of attention, from our experience of life to the ideas in our mind, has the effect of creating an invisible barrier between us and the world. For instance, when we see a car and the definition 'car' comes to the forefront of our attention, the particular qualities of redness and shininess which we initially experienced soon become forgotten. Not only does the experience of these qualities become obsolete, but when we only see the car through the 'eyes' of our mind (our i-deas) we often stop noticing that these qualities and details even exist. Consequently, we become blind to the life that we are seeing, even when it is right in front of our eyes.

The mind's 'best guess'

We do not solely use this cognitive shortcut to define the 'objects' that we see, we also apply it to our perception of people. In our everyday lives we use this same shortcut to organise and define the words, facial gestures and physical actions of our friends, family, work colleagues and even strangers. Our minds attempt to guess what we are seeing and re-present 'ideas' of what these gestures and actions mean. If, for example, we notice our boss walking around with a frown on her face, slamming doors and muttering as she goes, in order to define what we have seen with our eyes, our mind may immediately present us with the idea of 'anger'. Due to the lightning speed at which this idea is presented to us, it is common to also *feel* as though what we have seen, and experienced, actually is anger. This feeling often reinforces the strength and probability of the idea that our mind has presented us with. If we rely on this initial idea of anger to define our experience, it is likely that we will then start to create a further stream of ideas in the form of assumptions, judgments and beliefs, in order to make further sense of why we think our boss is angry – and so a whole story can quickly get built around our mind's initial 'best guess'.

Both the initial definition of 'anger', and the story which we then build around it, will inform how we choose to interact with our boss. After having surmised that seeing our boss slam a door equals 'anger', we might be tempted to put off the conversation that we had urgently wanted to have with her. However, unless we engage directly with our boss to explore further what our mind *thinks* we saw, the idea that she is angry is actually just a hypothesis. Until we verify the validity of our ideas and definitions they are not only in danger of being general and abstract but also untrue.

For instance, if we had decided to test our hypothesis by speaking with our boss, we might have discovered that the door had slammed because she was running to make an important phone call; the frown was as a result of worrying about her mother who, she had just been told, has fallen and been admitted to hospital; and the muttering was her repeating the name of the hospital so that she didn't forget it before she picked up the phone to speak to her father. Our boss was not angry at all, she was just preoccupied and in a hurry.

In this example, what could be seen with our eyes, was actually 'intense, hurried behaviour'. The perception of 'anger' was our mind's best guess at organising *what* it was seeing into a meaningful form – a form of meaning.

Unless we give our full attention to actually noticing the experience of 'intense, hurried behaviour' *as it is,* and make an effort to describe our experience without defining it, we leave our minds free to interpret our sense experience in a whole host of ways that are not necessarily true to the life that we experienced. Molecular biologist and author John Medina has used his lifelong interest in neuroscience to research how we can teach, work and learn more effectively, and in his most recent book, *Brain Rules*, John refers to the way in which our brain quite literally shapes our experience of seeing:

> Many people think that the brain's visual system works like a camera, simply collecting and processing raw visual data provided by our outside world. Seeing seems effortless, 100 per cent trustworthy, capable of providing a completely accurate representation of what's actually out there. Though we are used to thinking about our vision in such reliable terms, nothing in the last sentence is true ... We actually experience our visual environment as a full analyzed opinion about what the brain thinks is out there.[1]

Processing our sense experience into ideas of *what* our brain thinks we saw or heard is essential for our survival. If we had not evolved to recognise the threat of being eaten by tigers or the possibility of being drowned in a raging sea our species would have died off pretty quickly. However, our brain's tendency to fix, define and organise our experience into ideas it is not always helpful. As this brain function acts as a perceptual censor it can be extremely limiting and restrict us from really getting to know life *as it is*. The conceptual conclusions which our brains use to define life 'jump' into our awareness so prominently that our attention is directed straight towards them, and, as our attention can only be in once place at a time, if we are constantly distracted by the ideas in our mind we stop paying attention to the life that we are actually seeing.

When we remain unaware of this pole vault of attention from experience to thought, we end up responding and relating to our internal world of ideas *about* life instead of directly relating to life itself. This means that we fail to notice the intrinsic qualities, depth, details and uniqueness that make up life, and we stop seeing life as it is. This pole vault of attention also inherently restricts what we even think it is possible to see or to know, every single day of our lives. Iain McGilchrist, psychiatrist and author, writes about this way in which our brain automatically processes our experience in his seminal book *The Master and his Emissary*. From his extensive review of Western history, culture, and current neuroscience research, he writes that this processing of the brain:

> ... eventually becomes so automatic that we do not so much experience the world as experience our representation of the world. The world is no longer 'present' to us, but re-presented, a virtual world, a copy that exists in conceptual form in the mind.[2]

Henri Bortoft called this process of 'representation' the *'missed dimension of cognition in perception'*. The implications of this 'missed dimension' are vast and significant, both for us as individuals and for us collectively. As long as we remain unaware of the way in which cognition shapes our perception, we will only experience a vastly edited version of the world, one which, '... renders things inert, mechanical and lifeless'.[3] To overcome this cognitive habit we have to make a conscious effort to put our definitions of life to one side and to turn our attention to experiencing life *as it is*, right there in front of us. When we bring our attention to noticing the ways in which our brain tries to organise our experience we can start to move beyond its habitual definitions and expand our possibilities for experiencing and understanding life.

Edmund Husserl, the twentieth-century German philosopher, referred to this missed dimension of cognition as the *'naïveté of everyday perception'*. Everyday perception can be considered naïve in the sense that we are easily led into the belief that what we *think* is what we see. The switch of attention from experience to thought happens at such immense speed that we do not notice it happening. As such, we are usually tricked into thinking that we are experiencing the world, when actually we are only experiencing the thoughts that are inside us. This 'naïveté' which Husser referred to will continue to colour our perception of everyday life until we consciously direct our attention towards it, as it *appears*.

Aside from noticing this switch of attention in action, it is important to understand the nature of the universal ideas that our everyday perception 'uses' to re-present life. These representations refer only to the universal aspects of life and, at best, this is only one half of the story. They also have a fixed, black and white quality to them which sets the subject apart from everything else in the world. The severe downfall with our habit of mind that automatically brings these universal ideas to the forefront of our attention, as we saw with the example of 'holly tree' at the beginning of this chapter, is that these universal ideas are not flexible enough to accurately express life itself. All parts of life have universal elements to them but life expresses its *living* self through particular instances, each of which has a life of its own. Universal ideas, such as holly tree, car and anger, are true to life in the sense that they represent common aspects that distinguish one part of life from another, however, they tell us nothing of the unique form or particular expression that we are experiencing, or of the living context in which it exists.

Consider the millions of cars that are on our roads right now. All different shapes, colours, sizes, with different engines; diverse capacities such as speed, performance, emissions; and all being driven differently depending on their current driver. Even though each one of these millions of automobiles is different in some way, each one is called a 'car'. The same applies to parts of nature such as trees. Trees come in all shapes and sizes, they consist of thousands of different species, and each individual tree develops differently according to the part of the world, the specific location, and the particular soil conditions in which it is growing. No two are exactly the same yet each one of these diverse parts of life can be called a 'tree'.

If we are personally interested in trees we might notice the particular types of trees that we see in our everyday lives more often than those who just see them generically as 'trees', or if we have a love of cars we might pay attention to particular brands and models more often than just seeing 'cars'. However, to be efficient, our everyday perception tends to bring our attention to the most common definition of *what* it is that we are experiencing, such as 'cars' or 'trees'.

Unless we see something that is completely new or out of the ordinary for us, such as a neon pink limousine with a large cartoon pig on the side covered in giant sparkling gemstones, our attention will not dwell long in the world outside of us. As such, our everyday perception shields us from noticing anything about cars and trees other than the fact that we are defining them as cars and trees.

If we do not attend carefully enough to the way in which our mind evaluates and defines our experience of what we see, we are in danger of living in a kind of perceptual blindness, prevented from noticing the life that is right in front of our eyes. However, once we *have* noticed the existence of this habit for ourselves, we can begin to explore the ways in which it affects our experience of the world, and we can start to test its boundaries.

Seeing our mind in action

The most immediate way that I have had my attention brought to the 'missed dimension' of cognition in my perception is when Henri presented our class of MSc students with the picture below (Figure 1). Having been designed by his wife Jackie exactly for this purpose, the picture makes it possible for us to catch a glimpse of this cognitive process in action. Therefore, I would like to refer to the picture here, however, if you would like to go into further detail, I very much recommend Henri's book *The Wholeness of Nature* which is the original source.[4]

EXERCISE: ORGANISING IDEA

1. Take a moment to look at the picture in Figure 1. What can you see?
2. Try to describe the experience of what you are *actually* seeing right in front of you.

A precise description of the picture could go as follows: on the outer edge there is a thin black line which makes up the shape of a circle. Inside this black line there are a variety of different black, solid shapes, which are surrounded by white spaces. The black shapes come in a mixture of sizes and have varying amounts of room between them. These shapes all seem to have softly rounded edges and there are no completely straight lines.

However, we could also say that we can 'see' a giraffe! Or more accurately, that our mind is recognising, and thus organising, the picture into the 'idea' (a representation) of a giraffe's head and neck. If you have not seen the giraffe, spend some more time looking at the picture. If you need a clue, the head of the 'giraffe' is looking towards the right-hand side of the circle, and the horn-like forms on the tops of its head make up the largest black shapes at the top of the circle.

Once you can see the giraffe, take a look at the picture again and try to notice and describe the details of the image beyond the giraffe 'idea' that is trying to jump out of the page at you. Pay attention to the particular elements of the sensory data that the picture presents us with, such as colours and shapes. What do you need to do in order *not* to see the giraffe? Try turning the page clockwise ninety degrees, or experiment with reducing and increasing the distance between you and the picture. Is it even possible for you *not* see the giraffe?

When I have replicated this visual exercise with my students, we all found that once the 'giraffe' has appeared it is almost impossible not to 'see' it. The giraffe exercise is a clear example of the strength and conviction with which our minds define life into 'ideas' that directly alter our perception. Our mind guesses what we are seeing and sticks to it, quite literally. These sticky 'organising ideas' then become what we experience.

In this example with the giraffe, we 'see' the idea of the giraffe in such a way that the idea dominates our experience. The impact of the idea is perceptually blinding, it draws our attention so strongly that everything else seems to fade into the background. If we want to notice other aspects of the image beyond just the idea of the giraffe, we have to find new ways to experience the picture, such as turning the image at an angle or holding it very close to our eyes.

The giraffe exercise demonstrates, experientially, that there is more to seeing than meets the eye. It enables us to experience the way in which our own mind defines and organises our experience into an idea of what it *thinks* we are seeing. As we can tell from this exercise, the sensory experience remains the same whether or not we 'see' the giraffe. Those of us who do not see the giraffe are not being given any less, or differing, visual information than those who do see the giraffe. What is important to note is that the giraffe that we did see did not exist for us prior to our seeing it. It did not exist as a fixed, solid image that was already on the page (as the giraffe is not necessarily seen straight away) and neither was it a predetermined, finished image that our mind projected on to the picture (because the giraffe neatly blends in with the completely unique, random shapes on the page). We were only able to experience the giraffe once our mind had made meaning out of what it thought that we were seeing and once it had begun organising our perception in such a way that it could show us its idea of what the picture could possibly mean; from this process of combining particular sensory data with our existing knowledge, the giraffe-idea appeared.

In our everyday perception our attention is usually drawn to 'what' we see, or in this case, the giraffe, as if it were a finished object. However, it is our own way of seeing which allows 'what' we see to be seen in the first place. In *The Wholeness of Nature* Henri affirms: 'The *way* of seeing and *what* is seen cannot be separated – they are two poles of cognitive experience'.[5] The experience of the giraffe comes into being as our organising idea merges with the sensory elements to reveal to us what our mind thinks that this collection of black shapes *is* and what it means. 'What we see *is* meaning: we see "what it is" directly'.[6]

When I first studied with Henri Bortoft in 2008, the realisation that there is more to seeing than meets the eye completely turned my life upside down. Having experienced the way in which the 'giraffe' appears when Henri showed this picture to us in our MSc classroom, I began to pay attention to the ways in which my mind actively organised the parts of life that I saw every day, such as chairs, books, desks, houses, and trees. Then, once I had noticed the appearance of an organising idea, as I was experiencing it, I would challenge myself to see beyond it and pay attention to the unique sensory elements, whilst trying not to let the idea dominate my experience. By turning my attention away from organising ideas and directing my attention back towards life itself, I was able to recognise expression and dynamism in parts of life that prior to this 'giraffe' exercise had seemed flat and lifeless.

For instance, shortly after our week of lectures with Henri I found myself walking along a country lane in Devon and suddenly being able to 'see' the trees as dynamic expressions of life, as if they were snapshots of movement that had been captured on film, like billowing smoke clouds, frozen in time. Obviously, the trees themselves were not doing anything different on this particular occasion, what had changed was the way in which I was seeing them. I have always loved nature and marvelled at it, but it had also always felt very separate from me, as though it were simply a collection of still, silent ornaments lining a mantelpiece. However, when I started to turn my attention from the way in which my mind was organising the world and back towards my sensory experience, I suddenly understood how diverse the trees, bushes and flowers actually were. I started to see life as a series of unique, dynamic expressions of form rather than just a collection of static objects. Becoming aware of the naïveté of my everyday perception in this way meant that I no longer needed to just marvel at nature. I realised that by switching the focus of attention from noticing *what* I see, to the *way* in which I am seeing, I can actually learn from my experience. This way of seeing, which allows us to get to know life on its own terms, is what Henri Bortoft called a 'dynamic way of seeing'.

Our divided brain

When I teach I am always aware that speaking of 'ways of seeing' can appear to be somewhat abstract. Therefore, in some of my sessions I combine perceptual exercises with the ideas taken from psychiatrist Iain McGilchrist's work on the bi-modal brain in order to lead people into directly experiencing shifts in their cognition and perception. To illustrate the difference between the experience of responding to an organising idea and the experience of directly perceiving something *as it is* I often use drawing exercises.

Have you ever tried to draw an object and been disappointed because what comes out does not match what it is that you can see?

This occurs when the organising idea that is re-presenting what we see in front of us interferes with the action of drawing what *is*, as it is. What we end up 'drawing' is the idea of what our minds think we are seeing and not what we can actually see with our eyes. Therefore, drawing is a great way to experience just how difficult it can be to move beyond the idea of what we 'think' we know. It helps us to experience the simplicity of our mind's representations and to contrast the general nature of these ideas with the complexity of our actual sense experience. I will recreate one of these exercises for you here.[7]

EXERCISE: FACE/VASE DRAWING

1. Take a plain piece of paper at least A5 in size and draw a side profile of a face using a simple, single line drawing. Start from the top of the head, and finish with the neck. (Make sure you are drawing from your own memory, not copying the image below!) Pay careful attention to your overall experience whilst you are drawing.

2. Next, finish the outline of the face with two small vertical lines at the top and bottom of the outline, and then draw two straight, parallel lines, in the direction which the profile is facing. (See below for an example.)

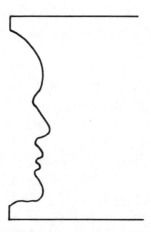

Figure 2. Partial Face/Vase Drawing. Credit: E. Kidd.

3. Now draw a mirror image of the face outline, using the parallel lines as guidelines to indicate where to start and finish for the top and bottom of the face (see Figure 3). Try to mirror your original line as exactly as possible.

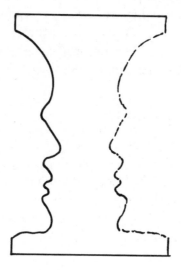

Figure 3. Completed Face/Vase Drawing. Credit: E. Kidd.

Reflection: How did the experience of the second 'face' feel in comparison to the first? For instance, try to remember if there was a difference in the speed you were drawing, in the type of attention required or in the quality of the lines that you used to draw each face.

In the workshops in which I have led this exercise the participants found that the task of drawing the first 'face' felt smooth and relatively quick to complete, as everyone 'knew' what a face looked like. The lines that were used to draw the first outline were mostly smooth, bold, solid and certain. In contrast, the lines that were used to draw the second 'face' were often lighter and much less defined, as we can see on the right-hand side of Figure 3. Most of my students reported that the second drawing task was a much more tentative, delicate experience and that a different type of attention was given to the task in order to accurately draw the second 'face'.

In the second part of the exercise, when we are copying the 'face' outline, we have to be much more present to the newness and uniqueness that is immediately there before us. We can no longer draw an idea of something that we already 'know'. Instead we must pay attention to what we can actually see in front of us. We also need to attend to its context, carefully comparing spatial proportions, and to also notice the relationships between the various shapes that the line forms, such as the shape of the 'nose' and the 'chin'. The experience of drawing the second face is often quite opposite to the first. The first face can be drawn quickly and abstractly. However, to draw the second face accurately we must be slower and more cautious, paying more attention to our sense experience than to our idea of what we are seeing.

This exercise is a great way to concretely explore our experience of attending to the world in two very different ways, depending on whether we already *think* we know it, or not. Each of these ways of seeing embodies particular qualities and characteristics that, according to Iain McGilchrist, are associated with the left and right hemispheres of the brain. Not *what* the hemispheres do, but the *way* they do it. According to McGilchrist the left hemisphere is the part of our brain responsible for *re-presenting* the world we experience based on what we think we already know. It gives a narrow focused attention that is associated with of the left-hemisphere of the brain in all animals. This capacity, for example, is what allows birds to hunt for small prey in amongst a vast expanse of complex woodland.

The left-hemisphere of the brain creates universal distinctions and separation *between* things. It focuses quite specifically on content and solid physicality. Henri Bortoft, following the French philosopher Henri Bergson, describes this content-specific, left-hemisphere way of seeing as following the 'logic of solid bodies'. This way of seeing defines, names, labels, analyses, quantifies and focuses on the separation of every *thing* that we see.

The way the left-hemisphere attends to the world is similar to the iconic tube map of London. The map re-presents actual routes and destinations in the city through easily recognisable, yet abstract symbols. We can use this map when we need to plan our route, to quickly find destinations and to navigate our way around the city with ease. The tube map is abstract yet it enables us to bridge the chasm between our limited experience of the physical space of London (which itself is constantly changing) and what we need to know about it in order physically get around the city, effectively and efficiently. The tube map of London is not completely true to the life of the territory that it re-presents as it does not accurately define the city in terms of how we actually experience it. In a similar way, our brain's left-hemisphere creates a map of life that is static, fixed and abstract. This way of seeing is experienced when we draw the first face in the Face/Vase exercise. The way in which the left-hemisphere organises our experience into abstract, universal ideas allows no room for uniqueness or difference and so its representations of life never accurately reflect our lived experience.

However, before a map of generalisations emerges from the left-hemisphere, we do experience the actual territory of life as dynamic, unique and alive. Our brain's right-hemisphere meets the world through sense perception, exactly *as it is*, without trying to organise life in the logical, analytical way of the left-hemisphere. The right-hemisphere of the brain allows life to appear to us in terms of itself, in unique detail. It '... underwrites breadth and flexibility of attention, where the left-hemisphere brings to bear focused attention'.[8] This 'right-hemisphere' way of seeing is experienced when we draw the second face in the Face/Vase exercise.

The way in which the right-hemisphere of our brain 'sees' the world has the effect of *presencing* the life we experience. This can be compared to getting to know the territory that is represented on the London tube map by actually going outside and directly experiencing the sights, sounds and other sensations that make up each stop and each line. As the right-hemisphere of our brain pays full attention to our sensory experience it allows us to engage with life as something that is always changing and evolving, without trying to evaluate or define it. As such, the way in which our brain's right-hemisphere encounters the world is participatory rather than controlling; in relation with the world rather than separate from it; enlivening rather than constricting.

What is important to note is that the very different way in which both hemispheres of our brain respond to the world must not be confused with *what* they do: 'These are not different ways of *thinking about* the world: they are different ways of *being in* the world'.[9]

Our right-hemisphere 'presences' the world through attending to our direct experience of it. It allows us to be in our experience, to dwell in it. Whereas our left-hemisphere 'experiences' life *through* the ideas and definitions which it uses to 're-present' life. When we are being in the world through our left-hemisphere it is as though we are stranded alone on an deserted island, even when we are in the middle of a crowded office, a dense forest or a busy high-street. This way of being objectifies, isolates and separates everything that we see, hear or feel in such a way that it creates a distance between 'us' and 'the world'. In contrast, when we are 'being in the world' through our right-hemisphere it is as though there is an invisible thread running between us and everything we meet. This connecting thread occupies the space *between* things, allowing us to touch the world and to be touched by it. This is echoed beautifully by the poet Mary Oliver:

> It is the intimate, never the general that is teacherly. The idea of love is not love. The idea of the ocean is neither salt nor sand; the face of the seal cannot rise from the *idea* to stare at you, to astound your heart. Time must grow thick and merry with incident, before thought can begin.[10]

A hall of mirrors

Iain McGilchrist suggests that, as humans, we have evolved into a pattern of cognition which allows the left-hemisphere of our brain to dominate our experience of everyday life and he believes that this has had the effect of trapping us in a kind of 'hall of mirrors'. When we rely on the abstract 'mapping' of the brain's left-hemisphere to spearhead our human existence, from the ways we interact with one and other, to the objects, structures and systems that we build, the left-hemisphere 'way of being' is reflected back to us in the world that we create. In western society we are quick to name, label, assume, judge and blame. We analyse and criticise in black and white terms, rewarding anything that seems logical, solid and certain. The ways in which we conventionally educate children today, including seeing them as vessels to be 'filled' with information, setting them regular exams so that we can tell them if they are right or wrong, good or bad, clever or stupid, reflects just one example of how the brain's left-hemisphere 'way of being' can impact the systems we create. This educational emphasis is not on genuine learning or understanding, but on preparing for children to be tested on what we, as educators, think we already know.

Another example is that in western society intellectual analysis and the ability to be logical and rational are considered inherent facets of being human and, as such, are commonly put on a pedestal, especially in education, business and government. As human 'ways of being' they are routinely regarded much higher than qualities such as kindness, compassion and understanding, which are often seen as 'nice' ideas but in reality, especially in professional practice, we generally regard them as weaknesses. In the West we also favour a type of logic that tells us one thing cannot be considered equal if it is not classified the 'same'. This manifests very clearly in the many discriminations that exist in our communities today such as sexism, classism, racism, and fundamentalist beliefs, whether religious, economic or political.

When we rely solely on our brain's left-hemisphere to make our conclusions about the world, we separate and abstract life from its living context, and reduce it to the sum of its physical parts. This has been very clearly manifested in the human systems and worldviews that we have created in our recent history, from the medieval mechanising of time with clocks; to the mechanistic scientific revolution; industrialisation; capitalism; and centralisations of national power and financial resources. Each example embodies a dynamic of extreme separation and individualisation, and involves the parts of the systems being treated as disconnected and separate from one another.

In turn, the qualities of this way of being seem to create a tendency toward competition and control. The division of labour is a good example. This foundation stone of industrialisation and capitalism led to a system of work which breaks each job down to its smallest part and then assigns tasks, such as sewing a bow onto a pair of knickers, to operatives who work separately to repeat these tasks over and over again. Josiah Wedgwood, who was considered to be highly innovative at the time, pioneered this approach in the UK in the mid-1700s, when he brought mass-production and specialisation to the art and craft of pottery. This remains the dominant model of employment and production today.

We have systematically explored the brain's left-hemisphere way of being, doing and creating in the Western world for several hundreds of years. I believe that we are all now experiencing the limitations that an over-emphasis on this inherently disconnected, life-excluding way of being brings, whether it be as a result of the credit-crisis; being witness to climate chaos; noticing the rising costs of privatised national services; record unemployment levels; or the limiting, mechanistic nature of a healthcare system which is focused 'primarily' on pharmaceuticals and quick fixes.

All of these examples reflect the use, and even worship, of the reductionist way of being of our brain's left-hemisphere. Iain McGilchrist suggests that in order to release ourselves from the hall of mirrors that we have created, we need to learn to practise a cognitive pattern that starts with the immediate, dynamic lived experience of the brain's right hemisphere, moves to the left to re-present it, and then goes back to the right again to create a broader, more contextual, living picture that is true to life itself. This means becoming aware of the ways in which our minds tend to fix and define our experience so that we can temporarily set those definitions to one side and then immerse ourselves in noticing our *experience* of life without them.

Sensing life

If we wish to experience our brain's right-hemisphere way of being we can experiment with giving our attention to our sensory experience, as fully as we can. By focusing on feeling the texture of a piece of cake as we bite into it, for example, or really paying attention to the sound of a piece of music, as though we are hearing it for the first time, we can immerse ourselves in our experience rather than just standing back to define it. Giving our full attention to our sensory experience, and really feeling what we feel, or seeing what we see, can help prevent our attention from being automatically led toward what our brain's left-hemisphere suggests that we already know about *what* it thinks we are experiencing. As the two hemispheres of the brain cannot function concurrently, paying full attention to our sense perception has the effect of quietening the brain's left-hemisphere, simply because sense experience is the right-hemisphere's domain.

We can open ourselves to sensing life any moment of the day. This involves pausing any internal dialogue that is occurring in our mind and opening our awareness to notice the way in which our senses can perceive the world, right here and right now. Sensing life is very easy to integrate into our day. It does not need to take our focus away from important tasks or appointments. For example, we can switch our attention from our thoughts to our senses whilst we are carrying out routine activities such as walking to work, sitting on the train or eating lunch. This can be especially helpful when we need a short break from our work, as using a narrow focus for long periods of time, such as concentrating on a demanding task, can be exhausting.

Letting go of our focus, slowing down our perception and allowing our senses to gently lead the way for a few moments gives our bodies and minds time to rest and relax. This open, receptive focus can notice our sensory experience, such as the warmth of the sun on our face, the wind in our hair, the noise of traffic or the colours of the trees, without needing to pay detailed attention to any one experience in particular. The exercise below gives examples of some ways that we can bring our attention to our sensory experience whilst walking.

EXERCISE: SENSING LIFE

1. When you are walking, whether it is to work, in the city, or in the local park, spend a few minutes gently paying attention to just one type of sensory experience at a time, such as sound.

2. Try to stop any internal dialogue *about* what you are hearing and quieten your mind's chatter. To do this consciously turn your attention to the qualities, patterns, and rhythms of the sounds that you are hearing.

3. If a few minutes is too long for you, set yourself an easier challenge, such as the length of the high-street, or the time it takes you to walk from the roundabout to the post office.

4. On different days you could pay attention to other types
    of sensory experiences. Experiment and have fun with
    opening yourself to sensing aspects of life such as colours,
    shapes, textures, or movement.

Taking time to quieten our mind and place our attention on sensing
life helps us to become more aware of the *life* that exists beneath our
mind's definitions and our organising ideas. By shifting the focus of
our attention away from our thoughts and towards our senses we can
move beyond our habits of perception and begin to rediscover our
own experience of life.

2. Rediscovering Our Own Experience

> Attention to the qualities of things resurrects the old idea of *notitia* as a primary activity of the soul. *Notitia* refers to that capacity to form true notions of things from attentive noticing. It is the full acquaintance on which knowledge depends.
>
> *James Hillman[1]*

First light

On a recent trip to the Island of Gozo, in Malta, I had the opportunity to go for a night hike across the island with a friend and watch the sun rise over the sea. In the small dusty village where our farmhouse was located there were few street lamps and as soon as we ventured away from their reach, the darkness felt thick and heavy. We left the sleeping village behind us and after a short drive started trekking through the arid countryside in what felt like the dead of night. For a while we were unable to see far beyond our own feet, the hillside was pitch black save for a blanket of stars in the night sky and we had to carefully pick our way along rocky paths illuminated by torchlight alone. However, soon enough the pinpricks of starlight gradually began to disappear as their inky black backdrop started to lighten and change colour, first into a deep, dark indigo, and then into the most magnificent royal blue. At one point the colour was so bright and radiant that the sky momentarily resembled a colossal lapis lazuli.

In vibrant contrast, the sky closest to the horizon began to glow with an intense, golden orange light, as though it were a gigantic smoldering ember. As the colour of the sky grew lighter the heavy grip of darkness started to loosen its grasp on our surroundings and suddenly life began to appear around us. The rugged stone walls that lined the hillside gradually became visible, and giant prickly pear cacti slowly came into sight together with the low-lying tufts of flowering wild thyme that emerged from under our feet. The vast Mediterranean Sea also started to reveal itself in the distance, delicately unfurling as though it were an enormous, shimmering magic carpet.

My experience of the landscape became noticeably more intense as the light continued to increase and everything that I laid my eyes on seemed to burst forth with life. Even before the sun itself actually became visible the island was already lavishly bathed in light and suddenly I realised that I felt completely alive. After having been immersed in the dark obscurity of night just hours before, the contrast of being able to see and to directly experience the life that surrounded me felt intensely invigorating. My whole body and mind felt alert and alive, able to fully sense life.

This encounter with the world at first light reflects the wonderful re-discovery of our experience that becomes possible when we focus our attention on intentionally engaging *with* life through our direct sensory experience, rather than being habitually consumed by our thoughts *about* it.[2] As the sunlight started to emerge, I was able to experience a rich diversity of qualities and specific details within the landscape around me. These features had existed in the darkness, but without light I could not see them. In every day life, when we habitually focus our attention on our automatic definitions and organising ideas, we prevent the 'light' of our awareness from touching the world outside us. This creates a kind of perceptual eclipse that covers the world in darkness and prevents us from experiencing it as it is.

In a similar way to the stone walls and prickly pear cacti that I was unable to see in the dark, when something has not appeared within our awareness, it does not exist as far as we are concerned. By turning the focus of our attention away from the inner workings of our mind and back towards our sensory experience of life we can lift this perceptual darkness and shed light on to aspects of life that may be new to us. In his poem *Auguries of Innocence* I believe the British poet William Blake described the illuminating effect that our awareness has on our perception when he wrote:

God appears, and God is Light,
To those poor souls who dwell in Night;
But does a Human Form display
To those who dwell in realms of Day.

When I was walking in the cool, summer air in Malta, the sunlight not only lit up the life of the world, it also intensified and enlivened my experience of life from within. Focusing attention on our sensory experience also has this enlivening effect. Attention positions and focuses the light of our awareness. This light allows life *to be seen* and makes it possible for us to deliberately reach out and touch the world with our senses. The more completely we give our attention to life, the more we illuminate the life that we are attending to; and the more light that our awareness shines on to life, the more qualities and details of life there are to be noticed. Giving our full attention to life turns up the brightness of our awareness, which, in turn, increases the intensity of our experience.

The alignment of our attention, awareness and sensory perception is what enables us to notice our direct experience of life and, therefore, forms a crucial part of understanding life in terms of itself and *on its own terms*. However, before we focus on giving full attention to our sensory experience, let us first turn to our attention towards experiencing the inner workings of our own mind.

From thought to awareness

In our everyday lives thoughts tend to slip into our awareness every waking second, commanding our attention and distracting us from the present moment. In order to rediscover our experience of life we can begin by conducting our own experiential exploration into how, and from where, these thoughts arise. We can do this by turning our attention inwards to notice our *experience* of our thoughts and to notice the 'space' (of awareness) within which these thoughts arise. The two following exercises provide suggestions for ways in which we can do this.

To start with I recommend that we spend five to ten minutes on each exercise before moving on to the next section of the chapter.

However, as we move through this book and begin to develop our capacity to pay full attention to our experience, we can repeat these exercises in more depth and detail at a later stage if we wish.

EXERCISE: NOTICING AWARENESS

Preparation: Sit in a comfortable position, close your eyes and try to clear your mind of thoughts. Aim to experience a silence in your mind, a space that contains no words, that is alert yet receptive.

1. All awareness is an awareness of *something*, so if we wish to notice our awareness we must first allow our awareness to touch 'something'. With your eyes closed, notice the ways in which you can be *aware* of physical sensations inside your body without generating thoughts. Spend a minute or so silently and curiously exploring a particular area of your body, such as the inside of your mouth. Focus on the way in which you can move your *awareness* around specific parts of this area, such as your tongue, lips and the roof of your mouth, to notice the different sensations that can be experienced within these precise locations, without using words.

2. Next, allow your attention to release its focus on one specific area and gently, curiously meander around the sensations in your whole body without noticing any particular area in great detail. Guide your awareness around your body at a slow pace and notice what it is like to experience sensations, and *to move* your attention, without needing to create thoughts about what you are doing or what you are experiencing.

Reflection: Take a few moments to review your experience of this exercise. Reflect on what it felt like to be *aware* of bodily sensations and to move your awareness around your body without needing to create thoughts about this exploratory process or the experiences themselves.

45

Now let us move straight on to the next exercise and turn our attention back to our thoughts themselves.

EXERCISE: NOTICING THOUGHTS

1. Close your eyes and hold an empty space in your mind as though you are intentionally pressing a pause button on your thoughts. Don't focus your awareness on any particular bodily sensation, just concentrate on experiencing an open, silent mind.

2. Now relax your focus and wait for a thought to appear. Sit quietly as though you were waiting to see a fish jump out of a pond, except in this case, your thoughts are the fishes. Rather than noticing what the thoughts are about, pay attention to the way in which they appear. Notice the qualities of how they come and go.

3. Practise alternating between consciously creating a silence in your mind and then letting go of that intention and opening your awareness to notice the thoughts that arise. Try to do this several times.

    Reflection: Reflect on the ways in which you noticed your thoughts appearing. Did the thoughts slip into your awareness gradually, gently catching you unawares, or did they jump powerfully into your mind? Could you see the thoughts coming, or predict them? Or did they just arrive out of nowhere? Also reflect on where the thoughts came from, did you choose to put them there?

Our thoughts are like fishes, they swim in a sea of awareness, but because they are so bright and colourful in comparison to the translucent space that they live in their obvious nature is what attracts our attention, while the existence of the sea (of awareness) itself gets overlooked. By spending time observing our thoughts as they appear, we can also come to fully notice the space of awareness within which they arise. Noticing the inner life of our mind in this way allows us to get to know thoughts in terms of themselves *and* to notice what the space of awareness itself is capable of, with and without thoughts.

Attention provides the spotlight for our awareness. When we pay full attention to our sensory experience our awareness can touch the world directly. However, if our attention is focused solely on thoughts about the world, such as naming a body part, instead of experiencing the body part itself, our conscious awareness only meets, and reaches as far as, the *thought* of the body part. When our awareness touches thought, and not sensory experience, we are temporarily disconnected from our bodies and from life itself. However, if we become aware of the way in which our thoughts divert our attention away from our experience of the world, we can make an effort to redirect our attention and attempt to more fully experience life.

I still find the experience of being able to direct my attention *without* needing to generate thoughts (in the form of words) quite surprising. It is almost as though part of myself expects 'me' to disappear when I stop having thoughts. On the contrary, the awareness that exists prior to our thoughts has a clarity and freshness to it that brings 'our' experience of the world directly to the forefront of our perception. The more we pay attention to experiencing the nature of our own mind, and to experiencing the distinction between thought and awareness, the more effectively we can explore the effect that our mind has on shaping our experience of the world. This puts us back in the control seat and places our mind in service of us, rather than letting ourselves become servants of our own mind.

If we wish to understand life in terms of itself, paying attention to our capacity to be aware without thought can aid our inquiries as it shows us that we do not need to instantaneously latch on to the definitions, associations or evaluations that our minds automatically present us with. This teaches us that although our thoughts are an intrinsic and crucial part of our experience, they are often part of a secondary 'meaning-making' process that attempts to re-present the life that our sensory experience first *presences*.

By noticing the distinction between thought and awareness, we can begin to rediscover, and focus more fully, on our sensory experience. We can practise this on a day to day basis by exercising our ability to pay full attention to our sense experience whilst carrying out simple everyday activities, such as eating breakfast, doing the washing up, or taking a shower. Giving our full attention to tasting the sweetness of our ice-cream, experiencing the liveliness of the soap suds on our hands or feeling water run down our body, moves our attention away from our thoughts and helps us to distinguish the difference between our ability to think *about* life and our ability to *notice* it, as it is, in the present moment. This focus on sensory experience wakes us up from the routine half-sleep that our everyday perception usually encourages.

When we give our full attention to sensing life we create the possibility to learn *with* life and exercise parts of our brains, and fundamental aspects of being human, that we would otherwise habitually ignore. We can start exercising these capacities and learning capabilities with something as simple as eating breakfast.

Eating breakfast

A dollop of wobbling, amber coloured orange marmalade sits quivering on my plate next to a golden croissant. The marmalade is gelatinous and translucent. When I taste it, I notice that each mouthful is both sweet and bitter at the same time. As I rip open the croissant the crispy, flaky outer layers crumble away to reveal the warm, buttery, spongy inside. A symphony of dark, earthy and exotic aromas float up from my coffee cup and arrive at my nostrils, calling for my attention. My coffee is syrupy, its liquid blackness is hot, deep and dark. As I sip the coffee while eating the croissant with marmalade, the contrasting qualities all combine, stirring an alchemical response within me. Once merged, the tastes become richer, deeper, and denser – the experience is far more than just the sum of its parts.

We may well remember having breakfast this morning but we probably both prepared and ate it without being aware of what our sensory experience of *eating breakfast* actually was. Maybe we took out a bowl, some milk and cereal – but did we notice our actual experience of eating and preparing our food? Or did the whole event just pass by in kind of a blur? Try to remember the last time that you really tasted something. When was it that you last paid full attention to what you were eating without digital distraction, such as a smart phone, laptop or television? When did you last sense a meal slowly and deeply, taking time to become aware of the distinctive textures, to savour the flavours, and to notice the unique sensations that occurred from eating those particular foods? The next time you eat a meal try to pay full attention to your experience of preparing and eating it. Notice whether your experience feels any different in comparison to a meal eaten without such full attention.

On an average day, instead of noticing our experience of breakfast, our attention is most likely focused on whatever our mind believes to be 'more important', such as reviewing our agenda for the day ahead, rehearsing difficult conversations, worrying about deadlines, or fretting about the fact that our partner left their wet towel on the bathroom floor yet again. The preoccupation with our thoughts during routine daily activities such as this is what causes us to end up spending our everyday lives in a kind of comatose state that zones out from the world and either obsesses over the past or becomes fixated with the future; either way, it ignores the life that we are experiencing in the present moment.

As an everyday event such as breakfast is often ruled by monotony and constrained by our hectic schedules, it is a particularly great opportunity to step out of automatic pilot. Each breakfast item such as the milk, the cornflakes, the marmalade and the croissant all express a variety of unique qualities that our everyday perception will routinely ignore. Usually we will only be vaguely aware of what the milk tasted like or the fact that the cornflakes crunched as we chewed them, and we end up left with a hazy blur of experiences that our mind bundles into one event and labels 'eating breakfast'. However, as a result of intentionally paying attention to the flavours, textures and forms with our senses, we can allow our attention to focus on one experience at a time and open ourselves to a much more satisfying encounter.

Once we have experienced that it is possible to *locate* our attention we become free to move it and to focus our attention on something of our choice. For instance, whilst we are drinking coffee during our morning break, if we notice that our attention is directed towards thinking about the rest of the tasks that we want to complete this morning, and actually all we want to do is make the most of our break, we can move our attention to focus only on the sensations involved in drinking our coffee and allow ourselves to really taste it and enjoy it.

Focusing attention on our sensory experience not only allows us to rediscover our experience of life, it can also have a positive impact on our well-being. In the fascinating book *Thinking, Fast and Slow* the author, economist and Nobel prize winner Daniel Kahneman, carries out an in-depth analysis into the different types of 'thinking' that we use everyday. As part of his research Daniel assembled a 'dream team' of specialists, including psychologists and an economist, to measure experienced well-being.[3] This team of researchers found that our emotional state is largely determined by what we *attend to*, but that whether or not we draw pleasure or pain from what is happening in the present moment depends on the *way* we attend to it:

> The mood of the moment depends primarily on the current situation ... Attention is key ... We found that French and American women spent about the same amount of time eating, but for French women, eating was twice as likely to be focal as it was for American women. The Americans were far more prone to combine eating with other activities, and their pleasure from eating was correspondingly diluted.[4]

If we want to fully experience life, we need to practise silencing our inner radio of thoughts and try not to fall prey to the outer barrage of modern digital distractions. According to John Medina, and his review of current brain science research, paying full attention to life also reflects the way in which the brain works best. In the book *Brain Rules*, he affirms: 'Multitasking, when it comes to paying attention, is a myth'.[5] Of course at some level our brains can multi-task, we can walk and talk at the same time – however, our capacity to pay attention cannot multi-task. John goes on to say: 'The brain is a sequential processor, unable to pay attention to two things at the same time. Businesses and schools praise multitasking, but research clearly shows that it reduces productivity and increases mistakes'.[6] Therefore, paying full attention to life, one task or experience at a time, can improve the ways that we 'do' our work and our everyday tasks, and potentially increase the amount of enjoyment that we experience whilst doing them.

Attentive noticing

Our direct experience of the world is a crucial gateway that we can each enter into in order to authentically understand the world around us, in terms of itself and on its own terms. Every part of life that has formed on this planet cleverly differentiates itself by expressing unique qualities. Each quality that a form expresses, such as the bittersweet taste of marmalade or the spikiness of holly leaves, discloses part of its 'language' of being (what it means-to-be that particular 'thing' in the world). Similarly to human languages, we can learn to 'read' these qualities, and discover the languages of physical forms, by paying full attention to noticing our direct experience, as we experience life. We can call this process of attending to our experience of the world as-it-is-*happening* 'lived experience'.

Henri Bortoft used to say that, for him, the biggest and most significant revolution in twentieth century western philosophy was phenomenology's 'discovery' of lived experience and of the primary role that it has in our perception of the world. Lived experience is our capacity to experience life, *as it is being lived,* in the present moment. Engaging directly in our lived experience is like dwelling in the hustling, bustling streets of the actual territory that is London, rather than living life by the abstract tube map of the brain's left-hemisphere. In his latest book, *Taking Appearance Seriously,* Henri describes the journey towards lived experience, '...most simply as "stepping back" into where we already are. This means shifting the focus of attention *within experience* away from what is experienced to the experiencing of it.' [7]

Experience is not something that emerges within a vacuum; all experience is an experience-of-something. By paying full attention to 'experiencing' something, such as the smell of our coffee or the taste of marmalade, the existence of 'lived experience' can begin to appear in our awareness. When we pay attention to experiencing life in the present moment we allow our awareness to focus on an unadulterated form of experience. This way of experiencing the world is not restricted by fixed thoughts, or limited by personal opinions, beliefs, desires or expectations.

The ability to focus our attention on noticing our experience of life is crucial if we want to get to know something in terms of itself. In the book, *The Thought of the Heart and the Soul of the World,* the American psychologist James Hillman refers to this ability 'to notice' life within the concept of *notitia*. '*Notitia* refers to that capacity to form true notions of things from attentive noticing'.[8] Hillman continues by commenting on the way in which habitually focusing attention on *our own* thoughts and feelings limits this capacity of 'attentive noticing':

> In depth psychology, *notitia* has been limited by our subjective view of psychic reality so that attention is refined mainly in regard to subjective states. This shows in our usual language of descriptions. When for instance I am asked 'how was the bus ride?' I respond. 'Miserable, terrible, desperate.' But these words describe me, my feelings, my experience, not the bus ride which was bumpy, crowded, steamy, noxious, with long waits. Even if I noticed the bus and the trip, my language transferred this attention to notions about myself. The 'I' has swallowed the bus, and my knowledge of the external world has become a subjective report of my feelings.[9]

Henri Bortoft believed that perception can only truly begin when we slow down. Our minds often work at an incredibly fast pace, jumping about from one thought to the next. As we have seen in Chapter 1 this can be very useful at times. It helps us to navigate our way through the day, efficiently and effectively. However, it also distances us from our experience of the world. Our modern lives tend to follow our thinking in that they too often become hectic and hurried, and we end up jumping from one appointment or daily event to the next. We rarely the take time to slow down enough to use the capacity of 'attentive noticing' that Hillman refers to, instead we are drawn into the thoughts and feelings of the 'I', which swallows everything up around it.

In contrast, lived experience is the process of *experiencing* life in the present moment, as we are living it. Bringing our attention to our lived experience involves *noticing* the think-ing of thought, the say-ing of words, read-ing of letters, eat-ing of breakfast, and so on. In so doing, this attentive form of noticing allows a true understanding of the world to emerge. The Scottish psychiatrist R.D. Laing also wrote about the importance of 'noticing':

> The range of what we think and do is limited by what we
> fail to notice. And because we fail to notice there is little
> we can do to change until we notice how failing to notice
> shapes our thoughts and deeds.[10]

Paying full attention to life, as we are living it, allows us to notice our lived experience – our capacity to *presence* life – before our mind re-presents it. We can stop and momentarily make an effort to notice aspects of life which we usually do not notice any minute of the day. These aspects of the world that routinely get left unnoticed include 'qualities'.

A quality is not *what* a part of life is or does, qualities are the *way* in which life expresses itself through physical form and behaviour. For instance, a rose expresses its unique 'rose-ness' through its own characteristic qualities such as, the silky, fragile nature of its fragrant flowers and the fierce, tough nature of the thorns which cover its woody stems. These 'qualities' are very different from those which other plants express. For example, a sage plant expresses its 'sage-ness' through the softly rounded edges on its elongated oval leaves, and the smooth, downy, fur-like feel of the leaf's surface. Both the rose and the sage have unique qualities that express part of their own language of being but if we wish to understand these languages we must use our full attention to notice these qualities, carefully and attentively.

To fully experience qualities we must explore not just what the quality is, but also the way in which it is being expressed. When our attention is directed solely towards *what* a quality is, such as a 'red' rose petal, we often miss the ways in which the red petal is expressing itself. If we look closer at this 'red petal', instead of just noticing 'red', we may be able to notice the velvety texture of its brightly coloured surface and be drawn in to the vibrant intensity of its particular shade of blood-red. These vibrant, intense, velvety qualities are very different from 'what' colour the rose petal is and, instead of telling us 'what' we are seeing, they point us towards the way in which the petal *becomes* what it is.

If we wish to understand life in depth and in detail we can use our senses to 'read' life's qualities, whether it is with people, trees, animals, cities, or organisations. However, it is often much easier to 'see' or to communicate *what* something is, than paying attention to the *way* in which it is being. For instance, if someone were to ask me what that plant is that seems to be running riot at the bottom of my garden my habitual response would be to say that the plant is a stinging nettle. If pressed for further information I might say that it stings you if you touch it and that it can be used in soup, as a tonic or a tea. However, talking about the stinging nettle keeps both of us at a distance from my experience of it and discloses very little of the stinging nettle's unique qualities or essential nature.

If I wanted to give an account of the nettle that is true to both my experience and to the nettle itself I would need to focus my attention on describing the qualities and form that I have directly experienced, as precisely as possible. For example, I have experienced that the nettle is much more delicate and fragile than its painful sting first suggests. The leaves are very thin and paper-like, and they tear easily. When I lightly stroke the stinging 'needles' outwards, from the stem to the tip of the leaf, I have found that they are actually very soft. The leaves have pre-historic looking jagged 'teeth' on the edges but this aggressive appearance sits in contrast to the overall elongated heart-shape that they form, which looks as delicate as it does severe. I have noticed that the pointed quality of the piercing sting seems to repeat itself throughout the plant, whether it is in the stinging needles that cover the entire nettle, the teeth on the edges of the leaves, the leaf's pointed tip, or the thin, upright nature of the stem. My sensory experience has shown me that the nettle seems to embody a paradox, a kind of fierce elegance, an aggressive delicacy.

When we live, and notice, life attentively, the unique living languages of life can come alive *within* our lived experience. Through engaging with something directly in our lived experience, it will gradually reveal itself to us. If we can perceive something – if we can feel it, see it, hear it, or touch it – whether it is in our body or mind, in our home or office, or in our natural or urban environment, then we can begin to learn its language. All expression that we can perceive through our senses *is* a form of communication, whether it is human body language, spoken words, man-made environments, natural landscapes, flowers, fruit or a piece of music.

Each quality that we notice is a snapshot of being, an instance of something being true to itself, and makes up part of what it means-to-be that particular thing-in-the-world. With time, patience and focused attention, these aspects of life are available for us to experience and to authentically understand – all we have to do is *notice* these qualities as we are experiencing them.

Focusing attention on our senses

In this chapter so far we have been looking at our ability to attentively notice our lived experience of life. Now we will go a stage further and really focus our attention on our senses by using a more precise form of sensory perception. Exact sense perception is a practice of paying precise attention to the experience of our senses in order to notice and be present to a part of life exactly *as it is*.[11] The French phenomenologist Maurice Merleau-Ponty believed that sense perception is a language that teaches itself, which is echoed by the German philosopher Hans-Georg Gadamer who thought that, '... being that can be understood is language'.[12] By using our sensory experience to perceive life as exactly as we can, attentively noticing the ways in which life is '*being*', we can engage in a process of learning directly from life.

The practice of exact sense perception involves using our full attention to notice the details of life that are available to our sensory experience, such as expressions of shape, sound, form, texture, scent, flavour and colour, amongst others. This includes noticing the 'quality' of qualities, such as the particular shade of a colour, or the unique tone of a sound. The details that we can precisely perceive will vary according to the part of life that we are paying attention to and some sensory elements will be more available than others. For instance, if we are perceiving an urban environment, sights, sounds and movement may be most apparent to our sense perception. On the other hand, if we wish to study a person as whole, beyond just their physical body, we can use this sensitive form of perception to pay attention to the ways in which that person behaves, speaks, acts, or moves. In this way, 'We cease from trying to grasp hold of the other person, to know him as an object, to work him out or to make him do things. We begin to let the other person be, becoming sensitive to him as a presence which comes towards us'.[13]

When we are practising exact sense perception with an aspect of life that at first may seem straightforward or familiar, it can open us up to the complex, diverse and intricate layers of detail, that prior to our investigation may have seemed unimaginable. In the workshops where I taught this method of paying precise attention to our sensory experience the 'revelation' of unexpectedly *seeing* immense detail in a place that we least expect it often bursts forth from the participants, creating a source of much awe and wonder. This 'surprise' encounter comes from the way in which life seems to suddenly *appear* when we use our senses, rather than our thoughts, to experience it.

As one of my students discovered, what starts out as a 10 cm square section of tree 'bark' can suddenly become seen as a whole universe within itself. In that particular workshop, I had asked my students to find a small part of a willow tree that they were drawn to and then use exact sense perception to observe it. One young man chose to observe a small section of bark on the tree trunk. He soon realised that there was a lot more going on within that tiny part of the tree than he had expected. He described that there appeared to be an infinity of detail contained within that one spot, which itself contained a myriad of colours, textures and layers, and was alive with tiny creatures. The part of the tree that the student had chosen to observe was no longer limited to his original definition, that it was simply 'bark'. Instead it had suddenly appeared so alive and full of life, that he likened that small spot to a whole, lively, interactive universe. The young man was so amazed at the intricacy and complexity of life that he had discovered in such a tiny part of the tree that he found himself overcome with wonder and curiosity.

We can each experience this shift, and enlivenment, of our perception for ourselves by practising exact sense perception. Let us explore this practice by first using it to rediscover a part of life that is immediately available to us, and often very much taken for granted, one of our hands.

Before you start this exercise try to consciously cultivate an open, curious, receptive attitude so that you can explore your hand from a fresh perspective. During the exercise, take your time and make a conscious effort to give your sensory experience your full attention. Try to explore the territory of your own hand like a pioneer, noticing and discovering things as if for the very first time.

Make sure to check-in periodically and notice where your attention is, observe whether it is focused on your hand or on your thoughts about your hand. If your mind starts to run away with itself consciously turn your attention back toward your sensory experience, and if your mind tries to tell you that you are bored, notice those thoughts (and any accompanying feelings of frustration) and then let them go. To keep your hand at the centre of your attention focus on the exact details that you can perceive with your senses and challenge yourself to continue searching for new details on your hand that you have not yet noticed.

If you would like to experiment with different ways of keeping your attention focused, one way could be to draw what you are seeing, allowing your pencil to record the experience of your eyes as they explore the surface of your hand. In this case, the aim is not to create a 'picture' but to help focus your attention on noticing exactly what you are seeing. In the insightful book *The Zen of Seeing* artist Frederick Franck called this exercise Seeing/Drawing. He writes that this type of drawing is, '...not self-indulgence, a "pleasant hobby", but a discipline of awareness of unwavering attention to a world which is fully alive'.[14]

Another way to focus your attention could be to write down descriptions of the particular details and qualities you notice on your hand as you progress through each stage of the exercise. Describing your experience as precisely as you can, helps to clarify, and provide a useful record of, your experience. Similarly to 'seeing/drawing', exact sensory description focuses on documenting the 'attentive noticing' that you are immersed in, and aims to describe details such as the slightly curved, horizontal lines that occur on the areas where the fingers bend, to help keep you engaged in a process of seeing ever further and deeper. Whether you are describing your sensory experience to help focus, or to accurately document, your process of attentive noticing, for the purpose of this exercise you do not need to include your subjective feelings or opinions about the practice, only note down the precise details that you are experiencing.

The exercise below comprises guidelines which aim to lead us into the process of exact sense perception, but they are not exact instructions as such. The overall aim is to get *into* the practice of precisely noticing what arises in your direct, sensory experience, so it is just as important to allow our own experience to lead the process. Read one guideline, find your own way into the practice, and then move on to the next guideline.

Lastly, whether you just look at and touch your hand, or whether you choose to also draw it, or to write down your observations, do not rush and do not worry about being 'right' or 'wrong', there are no fixed answers.

EXERCISE: ATTENTIVE NOTICING – SHORT STUDY OF A HAND

1. Choose one of your hands to focus on. Wiggle your fingers on that hand, rotate your wrist and view the hand from arms length. Allow yourself to get a 'first impression' of your hand and notice whether anything about it instantly catches your attention.

2. Now, slow down your perception and use your senses to immerse yourself in experiencing your hand, bit by bit. Bring your hand up close to your face and use your eyes to slowly work your way across the different 'parts' of your hand, such as the surface of your skin, your fingers, fingernails, palm and the back of your hand. Use your eyes like fingertips to feel your way around the details of your hand, such as its contours, lines, grooves, undulations, patterns and textures.

3. After you have explored your whole hand, find a detail that particularly catches your attention, such as the star-shaped, minute creases on the back of one of your knuckles, and allow your full attention to dwell in this

one area. Try to notice the tiniest details that you can perceive with your eyes.

4. Move your eyes very slowly across this one spot and compare the different qualities that these details have. For instance, notice the rough surface texture of your skin in contrast to the smooth lines; compare the deep indentations and the raised protrusions; or notice the dullness of the creases in comparison to the slight shine of your skin.

5. Now use your other hand to touch and feel the hand that you are observing. For example, run your fingers over the skin on the back of your hand and gently press down to feel the lumps and bumps that lie beneath the skin; work your way up the sides of your fingers and feel the contrast between the fleshy surface and their hard centre; or turn your hand and trace the lines of your palm with your fingertips.

Reflection: Spend some time contemplating the details and qualities that you noticed on the surface of your hand. Did you notice anything that you think you had not noticed before? Did anything you see, feel or experience surprise you?

Reflect also on the process of giving your full attention to your sensory experience. Did your mind wander or become frustrated? Was it challenging to keep searching for details? How did you have to change the way you would usually look at your hand in order to 'exactly' notice your sensory experience of it during this exercise?

This exercise could be expanded and applied to any part of life that we would like to experience, or to understand, in more depth. The part of life could be from nature, such as a piece of fruit, a tree, or an area of landscape such as river bed; or it could be man-made, such as a piece of music, a work of art, a building or a neighbourhood. The purpose of attentive noticing and exact sense perception is to disclose aspects of life, as precisely as possible. This involves paying attention to life as though the part of life we are attending to were describing itself. Instead of automatically explaining our experience, attending to life in this way makes it possible for us to reveal aspects of life that our everyday perception does not normally make it possible for us to notice.

The process of explaining life, which we routinely use to communicate our thoughts and experiences, does not show us what a phenomenon is, it actually diminishes it. As Henri Bortoft said in one of our lectures during the MSc programme at Schumacher College, 'If you can describe what is there, it appears'.[15] When we engage in a process of describing our lived experience, as if life itself were speaking, we bring the life of the world to appearance. This not only involves being extremely disciplined in how we notice and describe life, it requires us to turn our attention away from the subjective 'I' commentary that, as we have seen in James Hillman's example, has the potential to swallow a bus.

Paying full attention to precisely noticing our experience of life can be challenging, especially to start with. During my MSc research into the experiences of people who use exact sensory perception in their work or study, Henri Bortoft informed me that even he struggled with the type of attention that it requires. In one of my research questionnaires he noted, 'I am always trying to look for intellectual short cuts which will save me from having to refocus attention on the phenomenon through the practice of seeing'.[16] However, this is simply the dominant left-hemisphere of our brain fighting back and with perseverance we can get beyond its initial struggle. It is possible to bypass the fast-paced, impatient intellect with just thirty seconds concentrated effort of focusing attention on sensory experience, as I have witnessed in both my students and myself.

As Henri writes in *The Wholeness of Nature*, the redirection of attention away from our analytical minds that occurs in exact sense perception, '... actively promotes the restructuring of consciousness into a holistic organ of perception'.[17] By changing the way we see, and the way in which we notice the world around us, we are literally changing the way we use our mind. Therefore, challenging ourselves to think and to see differently is bound to feel at least a little odd at first.

Current neuroscience research has shown that focusing our attention on curiously exploring the world does have its advantages. Todd Kashdan asserts that when we engage in the world around us with curiosity, it can increase the neurological connections in our brains:

> Facts and experiences are synthesized into a web, paving the
> way for greater intelligence and wisdom. We become more
> efficient when making future decisions. We become better
> at visualizing the relativity of seemingly disparate ideas,
> paving the way for greater creativity. It is the neurological
> equivalent of personal growth.[18]

I also find that when I practise exact sense perception, richer and more detailed memories are available to me, long after the experience has ended. This 'noticing' aligns with current research into neuroplasticity and cognitive flexibility. Complex dendrite connections, which emerge in the brain when it links information gathered by different senses, create a more resilient memory that is more likely to last longer and be more easily recalled.[19]

In everyday life we can use exact sense perception to release us into experiencing the present moment or we can use it as part of an ongoing study with a part of life that we would like to get to know in more depth. This study could be of something that interests us personally, such as a plant that grows in our garden or the architecture in our favourite city. Alternatively, we could incorporate this form of attentive noticing into our professional work. For example, we could use exact sense perception as a tool to study the user experience of a product or service; to research well-being in our office environment; to investigate the effect that the experience of kindness has on people's day-to-day lives; or to study the lived experience of residents who live in a high-rise inner city building.

If we wish to study a phenomenon that *we* have not directly experienced for ourselves, such as the residential experience of people who live in inner-city apartment blocks, we can guide other people to describe their own experiences as precisely as possible. By reflecting on, and comparing, a series of people's experiences in relation to one another we can start to build an understanding of the phenomenon as a whole, even if we have not experienced it directly.

Reflecting on experiences, whether they are our own or those of other people, can bring an entirely new dimension to the ways in which we 'experience', learn with, and understand life. We will now explore how we can use our imagination as a tool to 'see' life in new ways and to deepen our understanding of the parts of life that have been experienced.

3. Imagination: A Mirror For Life

Skydiving in my mind

When I was in my mid-twenties, I travelled around South America for four months overland. I joined a group of other travellers and we toured together in a large truck. Apart from experiencing many new cultures and landscapes I also had the opportunity to participate in various adventurous outdoor activities. The type of activity varied greatly, from diving with sea lions in Patagonia, to body-boarding on sand dunes in Peru. I even had the opportunity to go skydiving in Argentina. We were staying in the wine-producing region of Mendoza for a couple of days and found a small airfield that was positioned between the vineyards and the Andes mountains. A local flying club was based there and offered skydiving at a much lower price than we had found so far on the rest of the continent, so a few of us decided to give it a try.

As I sat in my jumpsuit and watched the tiny plane take my friends off high up into the vast blue sky, one at a time, I was a complete mess inside. My heart was racing, I was shaking all over and generally filled with terror. However, when it came to my turn to board the plane and begin the steep ascent to 15,000 ft I was absolutely fine. A feeling of peace suddenly enfolded me, I was calm and fascinated by what was going on around me. Below us the majestic, sun-baked mountains of the Andes stretched out as far as the eye could see. Turning my attention to my immediate environment, I noticed the smallness of the plane, the fact that it had no door on one side and that it seemed to be partly held together by silver tape. This could have been very alarming, especially when my instructor had to lean half out of the plane door with me strapped to his back so that he could 'fix' something on the nose of the plane, and yet I wasn't scared.

As we edged towards the door and dangled half outside, waiting to jump, I started to get a little nervous, but it was nothing compared to the fearful pictures of myself that I had imagined when I was sitting and waiting on the ground. We jumped, or rather the instructor who I was strapped to jumped, and I loved it. The speed and intensity of the freefall descent was hair-raising but this dive passed quickly and once the parachute was open I felt so peaceful floating through the sky. I felt like a bird swooping gently through the air. The whole experience was incredibly liberating and I enjoyed every moment of it.

Before leaving the ground I had built up a picture in my imagination of how awful skydiving was going to be, but my actual experience was the complete opposite, I loved the flight and the jump. I often find that I create terrifying scenarios in my imagination prior to doing something new, whether it is teaching, public speaking, or even casually meeting a group of new people for the first time. This is a common experience and one that I am sure many of us share. The unknown scares us, yet our experience shows us that we often deal with it remarkably well. Our imagination can be our own worst enemy at times, exaggerating risk and amplifying fears, making up fictitious stories that have no bearing on how we actually *experience* the world. However, if we use our imagination as a mirror to reflect life, as exactly as we can, it can be used as a powerful tool to shine new light on our lived experience, and lead us closer to understanding life in terms of itself.

New ways of using our imagination

As we have explored in Chapter 2, focusing full attention on our senses allows us to notice specific details and qualities of life that, whilst caught up in our everyday perception, we would not normally notice. This attentive noticing makes it possible for us to experience a new richness, depth, and diversity in the life around us. However, these experiential inquiries into life do not need to end with our direct experience in the present moment, we can use our imagination as a mirror to reflect on our experience and to bring it to life again in our mind. By remembering and 're-picturing' our lived experience in our imagination, as exactly as possible, we can begin to notice dynamic processes, relationships and patterns that we may not have been able to physically appreciate with our eyes alone.

Exact sensorial imagination, a process that I was first introduced to at Schumacher College, is an exercise that can help us to notice these broader aspects of life and can be used as a tool to develop our imaginative capacities into a form of cognition. The process of exact sensorial imagination involves bringing our lived experience to life again in our mind, as though we are replaying a 'video' of it. By playing back to ourselves, as accurately as we can, an animated, 3D, Technicolor version of our experience, we can use our imagination to re-picture qualities, details and whole forms that we first observed through our senses. This sensorial re-picturing feels as though we are reaching out and touching the very life that we experienced, except that this time that life is *inside* us. Although sight is usually our dominant sense, when we practise exact sensorial imagination we can endeavour to bring back to life as many different sensory experiences as possible, according to those we used in the particular experience that we wish to reflect on. For instance, if I am using exact sensorial imagination to bring to mind my experience of skydiving, as well as remembering the visual aspects of the jump, such as the scenery, I can pay attention to the way my body felt resting in the harness, the dryness of my lips as we soared through the sky during our freefall and the peacefulness I felt whilst floating softly through the air once the parachute was open.

Using our imagination to mirror our lived experience in this way helps to embed the experience deeper within us. In his latest book, *Thinking Like A Plant*, the biologist, researcher and educator, Craig Holdrege writes, '...in perception we go out to things and invite them in, so in exact sensorial imagination we re-create and enliven within ourselves what we have met in experience. In this way we connect deeply with the world...'[1] When we use our imagination to re-member (put back together) a particular experience, as *exactly* as possible, in all its sensory and felt detail, not only can we deepen our connection to the initial experience but we can review the experience without the distractions of personal opinions, analysis, preconceived ideas or definitions.

In this way, exact sensorial imagination provides us with an alternative way of reflecting on life. Rather than using intellectual analysis to evaluate and to think *about* our experience, using our imagination as a mirror to reflect life makes it possible for us to continue thinking *with* aspects of life, even after the actual experience has ended. Exact sensorial imagination can also help us to notice aspects of life that we have *not* given our full attention to. Once we realise that we cannot *see* in our mind something that we were meant to be paying attention to, in our direct experience, our imagination soon reveals the gaping holes in our attention. For example, if we have been focusing on a plant, we might realise that we can't quite remember the texture of the leaf edge or remember exactly how the new leaves emerged from the stem. Or after replaying the walk to work in our imagination, we might realise that we don't know what the upper half of the buildings look like on a particular street. By getting a sense of what we have missed we can then attend to that aspect in greater detail the next time that we practise exact sense perception.

By using our imagination to mirror our lived experience we can practise focusing our attention inwardly and strengthen our ability to notice life in terms of itself. Arthur Zajonc affirms that five minutes, practice each day with this type of visualisation exercise is enough to strengthen our powers of concentration considerably.[2] Since each of us is different, and each of our experiences is unique, there are no fixed instructions for the exercise of exact sensorial imagination. We just need to pay full attention to our sensory experience of life and then try to accurately bring that experience back to life in our imagination. All our brains are wired differently[3] and, therefore, different people can re-picture experiences in different ways. You might be able to use your imagination to see the life you experienced in minute detail as it if were a photograph, or like me, you might need to recreate your experience by focusing on one detail at a time. Neither way is right or wrong, part of understanding life in terms of itself is getting to know ourselves, as we are. By curiously exploring and becoming aware of what it is possible for us to experience within our own imagination, we can use our own unique ways to re-member our lived experience.

Let's give it a try now. The sensory exploration of our hand (that we carried out for the exact sense perception exercise in Chapter 2) will be the experience that we draw on to practise using our imagination as a mirror. I have provided some guidelines for exact sensorial imagination below but, rather than following them exactly, the most important thing is that you bring your own individual experiences of your hand to life in as much detail as you can, in your own way.

EXERCISE: EXACT SENSORIAL IMAGINATION

1. Close your eyes and use your imagination to remember the sensory exploration of your hand, as exactly as you possibly can, as though you are recreating the original experience. You could start by remembering a specific part of your hand that you paid attention to, such as your thumb. Notice its shape, colour, or the detailed creases that cover it and then move around your hand from there according to what you paid attention to next, such as the palm of your hand or the side of your forefinger.

2. Go into detail and make the experience in your imagination multi-sensory. For example, try to re-live the experience of seeing the creases on your knuckles create rows of shadows, remember how it felt to trace the lines on the palm of your hand with your fingertips and to touch the smoothness of your fingernails. Experiment with using the 'eye' in your imagination like a fingertip not just to see, but to *feel* the surface of your hand.

3. Pay attention to your hand as a whole. Remember how it felt when you touched it with the other hand, when you rotated it and wiggled your fingers or used it to touch another object.

Reflection: How did the re-picturing feel in comparison to the actual observation of your hand? Could you notice certain parts of your hand more clearly than others? Were there areas that you realised that you had not paid attention to?

Exact sensorial imagination can be used to re-picture our sensory experience of physical form, such as people, places, objects, buildings or parts of nature, but equally it can be applied to anything that we wish to get to know more in-depth. The subject could be a mathematics problem, a challenge we have at work, an issue we are having with our partner or even a philosophical concept or an idea that we have for a new project. Henri Bortoft used to say that many of the physicists in the early twentieth century routinely used this type of cognitive exercise to help them explore theories and solve problems. Henri, a physicist himself, was a doctoral student of David Bohm (a well-known theoretical physicist who worked closely with Albert Einstein in the 1950s). Henri said that Einstein carried out this type of imaginative visualisation all the time and that people nowadays have forgotten about this practical way of using our imagination. During a lecture at Schumacher College he said, 'You can visualise things you can't see, until you begin to see them. This is how physicists used to work!'[4]

Animating our experience

The phrase 'exact sensorial imagination' came from *Exakte Sinnliche Phantasie* which was originally coined by the eighteenth-century thinker and poet J.W. von Goethe during his studies of nature. Goethe spent his life carefully observing natural phenomena such as light, plants and rocks, as exactly as he could. For many years he intensely focused his attention on becoming intimately acquainted with these natural phenomena by experiencing them directly. As a result of his long term, in-depth observations of nature Goethe realised that each time we interact with a part of life that is outside of ourselves we are experiencing simply a snapshot of its existence – one of many expressions that will come into being throughout its life. Goethe understood that in order to move beyond seeing life as a series of separate snapshots we need to use our imagination as a cognitive tool to bring the dynamic nature of life alive in our mind.

Nigel Hoffmann who was inspired by Goethe's way of seeing, calls this process of using our imagination to bring our experience to life 'Water cognition' and describes it as a fluid type of thinking that connects us to the intrinsic, dynamic processes of life, 'Like water, imaginative thought is sufficiently plastic and sensitive to take on the form of another being'.[5] By using this 'fluid' type of thinking we can begin to immerse ourselves in the 'unseen' aspects of life, such as the movement of growth and change, and intrinsic relationships and patterns, which are not immediately apparent to our eyes.

When we use exact sensorial imagination to re-member and compare a series of experiences it helps to bring the dynamic aspects of a phenomenon to life and, therefore, takes our understanding further than if we were just to consider each experience separately. By re-membering a series of experiences in which we have perceived the same part of life, on different occasions, we can begin to notice dynamic processes, relationships and patterns emerging *between* each separate experience. For example, if we have observed a certain type of tree at different times of year, such as spring, summer, autumn and winter, we can replay the experiences together in our imagination, one after the other, to bring the dynamic processes of the tree to life in our mind, as though we are creating an animation that is based on our actual experience. This can help us to begin to understand the dynamic and contextual nature of life, such as the way in which a tree changes according to the physical circumstances of its immediate environment and to the time of year that we observe it.

To get further into the way in which our imagination can be used to bring a series of separate experiences *to life*, let us imagine a 'flick book' of a cartoon mouse on the run. This book contains a series of separate images that each illustrate the mouse in a slightly different position, from one page to the next, and the changes are very gradual. Each drawing of the mouse is static, and located on a separate page, but when the illustrations are shown in sequence and at speed, by flicking the pages of the book, the images become animated. In this way, we start to 'see' dynamism and movement – even though the mouse itself is not really moving. Similarly, our imagination can be used to animate any part of life that we have taken the time to perceive with our full attention, over a number of different occasions. We can use our imagination to play these observations forwards, or backwards, to get a sense of life, dynamism and growth. In doing so, exact sensorial imagination builds the capacity to 'see' dynamic processes in our imagination.

For example, if we have been studying the growth of a plant we can use our imagination to re-picture the whole growth process from root, to flower, to seed, bringing forth our exact experiences of each individual stage of the plant's development, in sequence, one after the other. We can also bring our experiences to life in the opposite direction, imagining the various stages of the plant in reverse order, as though the seeds and flowers were disappearing back into the stem and the roots. This process makes it possible for us to glimpse the dynamic life of the plant in a way that is not possible through separate instances of direct observation alone.

We can bring the dynamic aspects of life to our awareness in this way with anything that we have taken the time to observe, such as a plant, a person or a place. For example, if we use exact sensorial imagination to reflect on our experience of someone we spend time with regularly it could help us to deepen our understanding of this person and to notice patterns in their way of being, such as the way in which they routinely change their attitude or behaviour according to the people they are with or the environment that they are in. On the other hand, we could use our imagination to reflect upon the personal and inter-personal aspects of our life. For instance, I have used exact sensorial imagination to reflect on, and learn more from, my past relationships. By recalling a series of experiences over the duration of a relationship, as precisely as possible, I was able to notice the habitual patterns of behaviour that had developed over the lifespan of the relationship. This process allowed me to shed light on 'invisible' cracks in the relationship that I had not noticed in day to day life. By using my imagination to mirror my experiences as exactly as I could, with sustained reflection I was able to trace those cracks right back to the beginning of the relationship. This process allowed me to see, with my imagination, what could not be seen with my eyes and to learn from my experiences in new ways.

In this way, exact sensorial imagination is an excellent exercise to extend and deepen our understanding of a specific part of life, and further our possibility of getting to know it in terms of itself.

Seeing colour – Goethe and Newton

In *The Wholeness of Nature* Henri Bortoft describes the way in which, by using exact sensorial imagination to reflect on his studies of light and colour, Goethe was able to notice significant patterns and relationships that had not been remarked on in the prevailing theories of the time. I will briefly outline Goethe's findings here but for a more in-depth account I recommend turning directly to Henri's text.[6]

By using his imagination to bring his direct sensory experiences of colour and light in nature to life in his mind, Goethe became aware that the colours red, orange and yellow always seem to occur together and so do blue, violet, and indigo. He observed that these particular colours appear to exist *in relation* to one and other, and can only be seen in these specific relationships. For instance, in nature, red light appears next to orange light but is never seen directly connected to a coloured light from the other group, such as violet. In other words, Goethe noticed that the particular colours within these two groups 'belong' together. Henri described this pattern of relationships as *belonging* together (as opposed to belonging *together*), in other words, the pattern shows an organic unity which emerges from *within* the phenomenon itself. Therefore, the 'belonging' that Goethe noticed between the colours is a pattern which is intrinsic to light itself, and even though this pattern is not a 'thing' as such, it is a significant part of what it means-to-be light.

The most popular study of light and colour that we attend to in mainstream culture today is the prism experiments that were carried out by Isaac Newton in the early seventeenth century. Although they are commonly referred to in order to 'explain' the relationship between light and colour, Newton's explorations did not uncover the relational dimensions between these phenomena that Goethe observed around a century later.[7] To understand why Newton did not see coloured light in the same way that Goethe did, it is first important to note that Newton did not set out to explore the phenomenon of light in terms of itself. Instead, Newton set out to develop a refracting telescope and to eliminate the chance of coloured light appearing when a person looks through the lens. To do this he used a prism as a tool to investigate light and is said to have demonstrated that light is 'split' into separate colours and that light is composed of coloured particles, which, when combined, appear white.

What Newton's theory actually demonstrated is that many colours can be seen to be reflected on a surface when a beam of colourless light is shone through a prism. However, these findings were interpreted by his contemporaries, and later followers, as showing the 'separation' of light into different colours. Using mathematical principles in combination with his theory of refraction Newton was able to assign each of the different colours with an individual numerical measurement that further enforced the 'idea' of their separation. However, the 'separation' of the colours exists only in thought, and in theory, not in lived experience. Even when experimenting with a prism the individual colours that Newton saw, together and in sequence, can rarely be seen alone by the senses, and are never seen alone in nature. The colours only became *thought of* as separate as a result of an organising idea of 'separation' which actively shaped Newton's findings.

As Henri Bortoft mentioned in an interview for the journal *Human Givens*, even the scientists of the time noted that Newton was 'seeing' the phenomenon through a theory that he had already constructed, and not through direct observation: 'Interestingly enough, in Newton's own day, nobody at the Royal Society accepted what Newton had done. They said, "You've got a theory hidden here" and told him what it was. The controversy lasted about 8 or 9 years'.[8] Newton's theory does not show us separate colours, it expresses a way of seeing (or thinking about) them *separate-ly*. The 'separate' nature of the colours is shaped by the mind and this particular cognitive interpretation of experience is then *explained* using a theory. Henri relates this way of seeing to the left-hemisphere of our brain.

In contrast to Newton's way of seeing 'separately', Goethe demonstrated a dynamic way of seeing that offers us a more relational approach to light, starting with the introduction of dark. Goethe believed that each phenomenon represents its own theory and so a 'theory' of light should be able to be perceivable directly in nature. By exactly perceiving coloured light in nature, and then using his imagination to bring these experiences to life, Goethe noticed that colours do not appear through the existence of light alone and that coloured light is only seen when light passes *through* something, such as the rainbows that appear when light passes through rain, or the coloured reflections that emerge on surfaces when light is passed through a crystal or prism.

During his studies of light and colour, Goethe investigated Newton's theory and observed coloured light through a prism for himself, by using it as if it were an eye glass. By doing this he realised that the coloured light only appeared alongside dark edges or boundaries; either appearing as a full spectrum, or as one of the two distinct colour groups, either yellow/orange/red or blue/violet/indigo. This led Goethe to believe that in order for coloured light to appear there must be light *and* dark present, not just light.

Light and dark

By repeating Goethe's experiments with a prism we can experience for ourselves the way in which colour emerges in the relationship *between* light and dark.[9] This dynamic relationship can also be directly experienced in nature. If we pay attention to the sky on a clear day we can see the pattern of colours that is expressed as a result of the relationship between blue, violet, and indigo, which Goethe called 'the lightening of dark'. This pattern of colours expresses the way in which the light that illuminates our atmosphere *lightens* the darkness of space. We can experience this phenomenon by noticing the way in which the colour blue intensifies vertically throughout the sky, from the horizon upwards. Starting as a very pale blue, which can appear to be almost white on the horizon (depending on the thickness of the atmosphere), the blue colour of the sky gradually intensifies as we lift our gaze upwards. When we tip our heads back to look directly up, as if staring into space, the blue can appear almost violet, especially when at altitude. If we are on top of a high mountain it is easy to imagine that the blue/violet that can be seen above our heads would become indigo and, eventually, as black as space itself.

The opposite spectacle, which Goethe called 'the darkening of light', can be seen when watching the sky at sunset. The closer the sun sinks towards the horizon, the more the colours in the sky progress from yellow, through to orange and red. Goethe believed that, 'There must always be some instance in nature where a phenomenon occurs in the simplest way possible, without any secondary factors to disguise what is essential'.[10] Just as Newton's theory expresses a reflection of a left-hemisphere, analytical way of seeing 'separate-ly', Goethe described the phenomenon as its own theory, through his dynamic way of seeing 'relational-ly'. Following the work of Iain McGilchrist, Henri attributed this way of seeing to the right hemisphere of the brain.

By paying attention to his direct experience of life, and then using his imagination to reflect on his experiences, Goethe has brought the authentic life of colour to our awareness in a way that Newton's studies could not. The 'Newtonian' view abstracts the phenomenon of light into a theory, while Goethe's way of seeing allowed the phenomenon to reveal itself, and made it possible for us to notice intrinsic patterns and relationships that a Newtonian way of seeing 'separate-ly' would not be able to notice.

It is not that Newton's discovery was not important. On the contrary, his analysis of the refraction of light led to the invention of the earliest known functioning refracting telescope. However, the interpretation of his experiments, which state that light can be separated into different colours, demonstrates that when we let our intellectual analysis dominate our investigations, our living experience of the world tends to be overlooked. This leaves us blind to the life of the world around us. Goethe's studies, in contrast, show us that we can only begin to fully understand the world when we direct our full attention toward experiencing life as precisely as possible, during both our lived experience *and* our time spent reflecting on our experience.

As a result of using exact sensorial imagination, Goethe allowed the patterns and relationships between colour, light and dark to appear and to come to life within his awareness. Patterns are easy to notice if we are told exactly where to look, such as watching a sunrise and noticing the red/orange/yellow group of colours or observing the sequence of these colours when light is shone through a prism, after we have been informed of their existence. However, when we are getting to know life for ourselves, it is only through reflecting on our experiences, and bringing them alive in our mind as precisely as we can, that we can begin to *see* these intrinsic, universal aspects of life, such as patterns and relationships, appearing.

Goethe's investigations into the nature of light and colour reveal just how truly interconnected, relational and complex life is. His work is also incredibly empowering for us as individuals because, as a result of being explicit about the way in which he attended to nature, and directly reached these insights, Goethe's studies are proof that if we too attend carefully enough to the ways in which we perceive and experience the world, we can get to know life in terms of itself. This opens up the possibility of an accurate understanding of the world to emerge through *our own* experience of it, as an individual, and the conditions for acquiring this form of *living knowledge* are not dependent on education, social standing or on the amount of money we have.

This style of learning through discovery, which Goethe's studies demonstrate, does not deny the importance of other types of knowledge and ways of knowing, but it does allow us to learn directly from life itself and, as such, it releases us from relying solely on external sources and authorities to give us *information* about the world. As a way of knowing it also offers us a crucially important pathway from which to readdress the relationship between thought and experience.

The same but different

Using our imagination to reflect on our lived experience can, as Goethe demonstrated, assist us in noticing the dynamics and inner unity of life. As we have already explored, these dynamics can include patterns and relationships which emerge between parts of life that at first glance, don't *appear* to be connected at all, such as light and dark. Another dynamic that our imagination can help us to illuminate is the way which life creates things that are the 'same', yet look very different. Henri Bortoft called this 'diversity in unity' (which he referred to in his earlier work as 'multiplicity in unity').

I have recently seen diversity in unity – the way in which life expresses itself as the 'same but different' – beautifully demonstrated in a photography exhibition by Leila Jeffreys, which documents the wide range of wild cockatoos that live in Australia. Her photographs each capture a single portrait image of a different type of cockatoo. Each bird that has been photographed outwardly appears-to-be very different from all the other birds, as none of them look the same, and yet they are all cockatoos. One cockatoo has a body covered in small, light pink feathers, yet its wing feathers are white and it has a Mohawk style crest on its head made up of longer white and orange feathers. In stark contrast, the body and wings of one of the other cockatoos is covered in black feathers with rounded tips that are much larger than those of its pink-coloured friend, and the head of this black-coloured cockatoo is covered in small yellow polka dots, which distinguishes it further still.

Not only do the length, colour and patterning of the feathers wildly differ but the cockatoos' beaks are also remarkably different in shape and size. Even when the images are placed side by side, these birds appear to be so different that had I not been told that the photographs were all of cockatoos I would never have thought that they were the same type of bird.

Coming to understand that parts of life can be the same, even though they outwardly appear to be different, starts us on the journey towards noticing sameness amongst difference. In order to develop an understanding of the inner unity that creates sameness, and the ways in which these 'differences' are organically connected, we can use our imaginations to compare 'different' instances of a phenomenon, such as these cockatoos. The following quote is from a lecture by Henri Bortoft in Bettona, Italy. It illustrates how this seemingly paradoxical relationship between sameness and difference can become a 'template for thinking intensively' and can lead to a way of seeing that is more attuned to the inner dimensions of life:

> 'Multiplicity in unity' means that there can be multiplicity within unity without fragmenting the unity because each is the very same one and not another one. This and other examples – especially the organic ones – can become 'templates for thinking' (David Bohm's phrase) intensively instead of extensively. I have found that by visualising these examples it is possible to practise switching from the extensive to the intensive dimension of 'the one and the many' and back again. My own work with this led to the development of an intuitive perception in which I found myself 'seeing intensively'.[11]

Our everyday logic usually stops us from noticing sameness in difference. This form of logic works well enough for identifying things that do appear to be the same, but if left unchecked this limited level of reasoning excludes anything in life from having contradictory qualities. For example, as this form of logic considers that a part of life either *is* or *is not* the same, it does not allow a third or 'other' possibility, and so it leads us down a path of exclusion, one that feeds off self-sameness and creates homogeny. This type of 'exclusive' logic, which equates 'sameness' with equality, can be traced right back through western history, especially in social circumstances. On a macro level, starting with the perception that indigenous or alternative communities are 'different', and therefore 'inferior', this view has led to the colonisation of the non-western world, and the development of exploitative practices such as slavery. Nowadays, this form of exclusive logic is currently occupied with propagating the same 'western lifestyle' in nearly all corners of the globe.

On a micro level, this cognitive obsession with sameness commonly leads us to reject anything in our lives that does not outwardly appear to be the 'same', leading us to think of it as false, a lie, not equal, or even to doubt its possibility of existing. If a part of life, such as a person, does not appear outwardly to be, or to act, the *same* as another person, or a group of people, then often we do not give them equal status. The resulting rejection of 'difference' occurs in abundance throughout the world today through the expression of discriminations such as racism, classism, sexism, and religious fundamentalism. These prejudices are external manifestations of a limited level of internal logic that does not understand diversity in unity.

The simplistic 'everyday' logic, born from the brain's left-hemisphere way of being, turns the world into a collection of 'objects' by freezing them in time, separating, isolating them and abstracting one from the other in our mind. In the process it blinds us to the existence of inner unity (intrinsic connections and relationships) and therefore squeezes the livingness out of life. In his intriguing book, *Meditation as Contemplative Inquiry*, Arthur Zajonc, a professor of Physics at Amherst College and director at the Center for Contemplative Mind in Society, points to the limitations of this logic in his writing on 'true openness':

> The catastrophes of ethnic conflict are only the extension
> of a myopia that sees the world from one vantage point
> and can only judge the world against one background, our
> own. Considered in this way, true openness is one of the
> most important intellectual and moral accomplishments to
> which we can aspire. In the realm of ideas it is required for
> discovery, but in the conduct of human affairs it is essential
> to our very humanity.[12]

To expand our understanding of life beyond this limited form of logic we can use exact sensorial imagination to discover and experience the dynamic of 'diversity in unity' and to shed light on the intrinsic connections between parts of life that are invisible to our eyes. By using our imagination to bring instances of life, such as the photographs of different cockatoos, in our mind we can learn to challenge the clear, finite borders that we often perceive as separating sameness and difference. We could do this with any part of life that we have given our full attention to, such as plants, animals, clouds, rocks or whole areas of different landscapes.

On the other hand, to directly explore aspects of 'sameness' and 'difference' in a social and humanitarian context, we could use exact sensorial imagination to explore the connections between ourselves and other people. For example, we can use our imagination to study ourselves in relation to another person who we do not consider to be our equal. This person could be someone we do not approve of; a person who we perceive to be more or less worthy, intelligent, likeable or attractive than ourselves; or it could be a person of a different sexual orientation, gender, culture or religion. The aim of the exercise is not to judge ourselves for perceiving inequality, but to openly and honestly explore the *differences* that we think make us unequal.

EXERCISE: DIVERSITY IN UNITY

1. Use your imagination to picture aspects of a person that you perceive to be different from yourself, and consider unequal, in some way. These aspects could include their physical shape and form, lifestyle, personality, behaviour or their values.

2. In order to bring these 'differences' to expression, try to re-picture not just *what* this person does, but the *way in which* they do it. For instance, if you perceive this person to be arrogant, use your imagination to explore the exact way in which they express that arrogance, such as appearing to be distant and disconnected to when they interact with people, or acting as though they are better than those around them.

3. After focusing on these 'differences' turn your attention to re-picturing any *similarities* between you, these could be physiological, behavioural, situational, emotional or

intellectual. For are a start, you are both human and need to eat, drink and sleep to survive, but maybe you also both live in the same city, are the same sex, or drive the same car. Or maybe you both live alone, or work in a stressful environment.

4. Now notice whether there are any times in your life when you have expressed yourself in a similar way to this person, in your behaviour or your lifestyle. For instance, maybe you acted arrogantly when you were a teenager or have your own set of beliefs that you feel certain are 'correct'.

Reflection: Spend a few minutes contemplating your understanding of sameness and difference in relation to yourself and the person who you considered to be unequal. In which ways are you the same as them? How are you different from them? Is there anything that connects, or relates you each other physically, socially, culturally? Are the ways in which you are both the same, or different, noticeable externally, or connected to your inner lives?

In contrast to the factory line logic of 'sameness' that the left-hemisphere of the brain uses to organise our experience of the world, life is actually created by countless complex processes and dynamics that lead it to express itself the *same but differently*. This simultaneous and interconnected way in which sameness and difference appear presents a paradox to the logic of our everyday perception, yet this dynamic is true to the way in which life expresses and differentiates itself. Henri Bortoft called this form of living logic 'self-differencing'.

Developing our imagination as a form of cognition can help us to craft our mind into a tool that is as alive and fluid as the dynamics of life itself. In doing so, we can begin to overcome the illusion of separation that our minds, organisations and societies have created, and start to notice the intrinsic relationships, patterns and inner unity which provide proof of the ways in which *all* people, places and parts of nature are, in some way, the 'same but different'.

4. Understanding Wholeness

For me the camera is a sketchbook, an instrument of intuition and spontaneity, the master of the instant which, in visual terms, questions and decides simultaneously.

Henri Cartier-Bresson[1]

Photographing life in Hong Kong

Hong Kong is a fantastic place for sensing life as the streets are always alive. In the daytime the roads burst full with people, cars, buses, and iconic red taxis. At night, bright neon signs infuse the city with a vibrant artificial life that keeps the streets animate and awake 24/7. On the pavements of the densely built city, every nook and cranny is filled with the efforts of people trying to make a living. When I lived in Hong Kong these endeavours ranged from dai pai dongs, which were makeshift street stands that sold cooked food to office workers, to a multitude of small family run stores that specialised in selling specific local items such as tied crabs or Chinese medicine. There were even tiny improvised workplaces set up in narrow back alleys. These rough and ready enterprises were squeezed into the tiniest of spaces and often run by a lone elderly person, such as the man who busily mended shoes and umbrellas close to where I used to live on Hong Kong Island. Not only were the streets alive but the air was full of life too. The city was always filled with pungent smells such as the sweet scent of incense floating out of temple doors or the heady mixture of peculiar aromas that wafted out of shops selling local produce, such as dried fish and durian fruit. Up close, life on the ground in Hong Kong was full, fast and intense in every way possible, it was a hive of activity.

Despite the personal and ethical issues that I struggled with whilst living in this vast city, I was fascinated by it and spent a lot of time walking around, just taking life in. My interest in photography gave me even more reasons to wander the city. On one particular occasion I took a day off work and went out to take photographs for an annual photography competition that was hosted by *BC Magazine*, a Hong Kong based English-language magazine. The theme of the competition the year I entered was 'Life in Hong Kong' and the aim was to take a photograph that best expressed the nature of life in the city. It was quite a challenge to get the 'whole' of Hong Kong life summed up in one shot. There were too many diverse parts that make life there what it is, such as the markets, temples, taxis, skyscrapers, ferries, giant shopping malls, beaches, the harbour – the list was endless. I felt as though I couldn't possibly fit enough of these distinct parts into one shot to represent the *whole* life of the city. However, when I observed the city from a distance, the essential nature and life of it seemed to somehow get lost, and so I spent the entire day immersing myself in the sights and sounds that surrounded me.

Eventually, the photograph that I submitted for the competition was taken whilst I was riding on one of the Star Ferries. These iconic ancient ferries, some of which have been in use since the late 1950s, provide a passenger service between Hong Kong Island and Kowloon. They are one of the few historic relics left surviving in the city. The open-sided ferries are painted white and green, and their top decks are filled with rows of wooden seats that each have a star carved into them. There are much faster ways to cross the harbour, but the Star Ferry allows for a more satisfying experience. I used to enjoy sitting next to the open-sides, inhaling the humid, salty sea air and watching as the ferries courageously dodged the gigantic container ships which also passed through the harbour.

On that particular day, as the ferry left Kowloon I noticed an older gentleman on the opposite side of the boat to me. He was alone on his row of seats and sat next to the edge of the boat looking out towards the towering IFC building on Hong Kong Island. While the scene captivated my attention my intuition struck. I suddenly had an internal sense that what I was experiencing before me was an authentic expression of 'Life in Hong Kong' and so I used my SLR camera to capture the moment. Somehow the essential nature of Hong Kong life was expressing itself through that tiny part of time and space that I was individually experiencing – the lone gentleman, the ferry, the harbour, Hong Kong island and its skyscrapers, they all came together in one insightful flash, an 'aha' moment, that was far more than the sum of its parts. I didn't need to think consciously about this process at the time, the impulse just struck me and I responded by documenting it in film.

I called the photograph '1 in 7 million' and it won the photography competition. Winning the competition affirmed my intuition that this photograph expressed, through a single image, a part of 'Life in Hong Kong' as a whole. The photograph was judged by a group of people totally separate from me, and from my experience, but despite this separation they too understood the 'wholeness' that I had perceived in that flash of insight on the ferry. The famous French photographer Henri Cartier-Bresson called this process of instantaneously capturing intuition through photography the 'decisive moment'. It is a moment where the essential nature of an experience is intuited and recorded simultaneously. He believed that this involves, '...putting one's head, one's eye, and one's heart on the same axis'.[2]

Although intuition is commonly seen as simply a personal experience, regarded as relative and relevant only to the individual, the decisive moment that I had intuited by aligning my 'head, eye and heart', expressed something more than a mere recording of my subjective experience. The consensus that arose between the judging panel suggests that there was a universal nature associated with the life that was expressed within the photograph, something which consisted not only of my personal interpretation, but that was also true to the life of Hong Kong itself.

Opening our attention

In order to experience whole, authentic examples of Hong Kong life expressing itself, I allowed my attention and my senses to open and step 'right into the parts'. To accomplish this I alternated between the focused attention of my direct sensory experience and the open attention of my intuition. Intuition, which is also called non-inferential perception, represents our human capacity to 'read between the lines'. It enables us to understand intrinsic meaning and significance without it being inferred or physically spelt out in front of us (as though the meaning that we perceived was itself an object).

In order to allow an intuitive insight to arise, we have first to give our full attention to our experience in the present moment. The action of fully focusing on our experience, rather than our thoughts, has the effect of taking us outside 'ourselves' and connecting us directly to the world. Once this connection has been established, we can then release the specific focus of our attention and open our awareness, so that we remain present to our experience yet not fixated on it. This keeps the connection between us and the world alive, yet frees up our intuition to sense life in its own unique way.

The open attention that is needed for intuitive insight to emerge is different from the focused attention that is required by exact sense perception. Open attention also remains both active *and* receptive but rather than focusing on the individual parts of a person, a plant or a problem, the openness creates a space within us, in order to tend to our experience of these expressions of life as a *whole*.

The experience of 'open attention' feels as though we are witnessing a part of life, rather than inspecting it – a little like gazing at Monet's painting of water lilies and allowing our eyes to saunter across it, rather than specifically focusing on noticing the exact brush strokes that make up a particular shadow. Allowing our attention to open does not mean that we can let our mind wander, if we do our attention is likely to follow it and we will disconnect from the painting. Alternatively, by paying attention to the painting, while releasing the need to be focused on particulars, we can open ourselves to the 'whole' experience. Nigel Hoffmann describes the open attention given at this intuitive stage of inquiry (which he calls 'Air cognition') as 'receptive will'. He writes that:

> 'Receptive will' occurs through a conscious participation
> in the phenomenon, already developed at the Water stage,
> in a way that allows researchers to 'offer their thinking to
> nature so that nature can think in them.'[3]

When we complement and intersperse our focused attention with this open attention we create a space for the essential nature and characteristic qualities of a phenomenon to appear within us.

Examples of this intuitive perception include the 'understanding' that emerges from within us whilst we are reading a book or suddenly 'seeing' the missing link in a problem at work that has been puzzling us for days. These intrinsic aspects of life cannot be outwardly perceived using our senses, yet it is the experience of our senses that can lead us toward them. In his book, *Meditation as Contemplative Inquiry,* Arthur Zajonc describes the movement between open and focused attention as it occurs in meditation:

> In meditation we move between focused and open
> attention. We give our full attention to the individual
> words of our chosen text, and to their associated images
> and meanings. Then we move to their relationship
> with each other so that a living organism of thought
> is experienced ... After a period of vivid concentration
> on the content of meditation, the content is released.
> That which was held is gone. Our attention opens. We
> are entirely present. An interior psychic space has been
> intently prepared, and we remain in that space. We wait,
> not expecting, not hoping, but present to welcome
> whatever may or may not arise within infinite stillness.
> If a shy, dawning experience emerges into the space we
> have prepared, then we gratefully and gently greet it: not
> grasping, not seeking.[4]

Focused attention deals with the realm of all that is immediately perceptible and uses our senses to reach out towards things, such as the colour of the mug on our desk, the churning feeling in our stomach, or the sound of sirens floating in through our office window. By contrast, an intuitive insight is an understanding of something which is outside of us, but the insight arises within our open attention, as if it has come towards us. This intuitive insight, or understanding, is an intrinsic part of what we are observing but it is not of our own creation in a subjective sense.

Wrapping our minds around this concept can feel as though we are performing some kind of mental tongue twister. This is because intuitive insights seem to emerge in a way that is quite the reverse from the way in which we ordinarily employ our senses to perceive the world. With focused sensory perception we narrow our gaze and shoot the arrow of our attention towards an exact target, whereas with intuitive perception, we hold the focus of our inquiry with a loose gaze and open our attention, as though we are creating an internal target board which the life outside of us can use for the projection of its own arrows.

When engaged in getting to know a part of life, intentionally putting our intuitive capacities into practice is not as straightforward as the direct ways by which we can put our thoughts and senses into immediate action. As with firing an arrow, the processes of thinking and sensing involve turning our awareness in a forward direction towards something that, once our awareness touches it, we can instantly experience. By contrast, exercising our intuitive capacity does not guarantee an experience in such an immediate way, it involves more of a waiting game and usually consists of what the world wants to show us, rather than what we specifically want to see.

In one sense, intuition involves a degree of losing ourselves, it requires us to let go of our direct will 'to do', or 'to be', in a certain way. Using our intuitive capacities on command might not be straightforward but we can put open attention into practice everyday. When we are faced with a problem at home, trying to overcome a challenge at work or maybe attempting to get to know our co-workers, our city, or our local countryside more deeply, instead of only directing our attention to focus on specific aspects of these examples, we can also spend time opening our awareness whilst still paying attention to their presence. We could try practising open attention whilst walking to work, or strolling through the woods in our local park, allowing our awareness to gently meander over the whole of our surroundings without letting it focus intently on specific details.

Through experimenting with using, and alternating between, focused and open attention in a variety of everyday situations we can start to *experience* the differences between them for ourselves. For instance, allowing ourselves to be moved by the experience of a sunset and letting the whole scene come alive within the openness of our awareness, feels very different than if we were to view the same sunset, yet use our focused attention to precisely note the specific colours and qualities of the clouds in the sky.

The 'shy, dawning experience' that Arthur Zajonc referred to is an example of what can emerge within open attention. This description also illustrates the way in which intuitive perceptions tend to come *upon us*, rather than occurring exactly as and when we want them to. When an intuitive insight arises it often doesn't come in the form of words and is more likely to be a feeling, a physical sensation, an image or a sudden understanding, similar to the 'aha' moment that I perceived when taking that photograph on the Star Ferry. As such, these insights can be quite hard to describe.

For intuition to be understood, we must experience it and there is no set of fixed instructions that will guarantee successful results. All we can do is try to create the conditions within ourselves for intuitive understanding to emerge. We can use the exercise below to practise a sequence of focusing and opening our attention. Once we have done this particular exercise we can then use the experience we gain from it to guide the same process in other aspects of our lives.

EXERCISE: OPEN ATTENTION

1. Read the poem below, slowly, with care and full attention.

2. Then read the poem once more as if the words were alive and you could see, feel and touch everything they say.
    (It might help to imagine that you are an actor on stage performing the poem to a live audience.)

3. Next, close your eyes and use your imagination to focus on re-living your experience of the poem, as exactly as possible.

4. Finally, let go of this focus and take a few minutes to create a quiet stillness within. Empty your mind and don't expect anything particular to arise, just practise being open. Try not to seek or to grasp, but do notice any feelings, images or particular words that come to mind.

'Leisure' by William Henry Davies

> *What is this life, if full of care,*
> *We have no time to stand and stare.*
> *No time to stand beneath the boughs,*
> *And stare as long as sheep or cows.*
> *No time to see, when woods we pass,*
> *Where squirrels hide their nuts in grass.*
> *No time to see, in broad daylight,*
> *Streams full of stars, like skies at night.*
> *No time to turn at Beauty's glance,*
> *And watch her feet, how they can dance.*
> *No time to wait till her mouth can,*
> *Enrich that smile her eyes began.*
> *A poor life this, if full of care,*
> *We have no time to stand and stare.*

Reflection: Spend a few moments reflecting on the difference between focusing on experiencing the words, and letting the words go to allow the whole poem to settle within you. Once you had absorbed and let go of the words, were there any impressions left inside your mind or did any feelings, images or thoughts emerge? How did it feel to 'open' your attention?

When we give our open attention to life, with enough patience and practice, we might reach a stage when, without us having to say anything, the life before us may well 'say' something back. This is not to say that all of our intuitive insights will be correct. To allow ourselves to become genuine instruments for understanding life we must constantly refine our ability to discern what is and is not of our own making. We can strengthen the validity of our intuition by dedicating time to getting to know parts of life, and most crucially coming to know ourselves, ever further and deeper.

Experiencing wholeness

Wholeness is the essential nature of what it *means-to-be* something. It exists within, and is fundamental to, life itself, yet it is not physically laid out before us as if it were a 'whole' object. Wholeness is no-*thing*, but not nothing. Henri Bortoft referred to it as an 'active absence', as it is ever-present and everywhere, but never entirely present in physical form, and therefore is invisible to our everyday perception.

Wholeness is intrinsically embedded in all parts of nature but instead of presenting itself in its entirety, it expresses itself *through* the parts that make up whole forms. In this way, wholeness could be seen as life's unique signature and certificate of authenticity, all rolled into one. It is what gives an apple tree its qualities of apple-ness; what distinguishes Monet's paintings from all other works of art; what makes an oak tree an 'oak' and an ash tree an 'ash'.

Wholeness is what gives life meaning and substance, and prevents life from being arbitrary and superficial, both in nature and in the creation of human artefacts. As wholeness is an inner dimension of life, it follows that we must use our own inner dimensions to perceive it. Intuition is, as we have already explored, one such capacity. In modern society we often have trouble dealing with the concepts of intuition and wholeness. Our brain's dominant left-hemisphere style of thinking dwells in a 'solid' form of reality that understands the world as a collection of formed, finished objects, each separate from the other. This means that when we try to *think* about intuitive insights, or our ability to perceive the 'inner' dimensions of the world such as wholeness, these aspects of life can seem rather bizarre, abstract or mysterious, even if we ourselves have experienced them. However, our intuitive capacity is neither bizarre nor full of mystery, we actually use it to perceive the essential nature, or *wholeness*, of life every single day. The process of 'understanding' is one such example.

Understanding shows itself, and comes into being, as a result of the process of bringing forth meaning. Consider the experience of understanding a story. We place our focus outside ourselves to perceive the words of the story with our senses and, as such, the initial focus of our attention is towards the world, whether moving our eyes like fingers to trace an unfolding trail of words on a page, or using our ears to follow the thread of words being spoken. As we move from word to word, and sentence to sentence, taking each one inside us before momentarily pausing to let each one go, it is only then that the meaning of the story as a *whole* gradually begins to emerge within us.

The meaning of a story is not physically sense-perceptible as a whole, as if it were a separate entity or object placed amongst the words. We cannot *see* the story, but we can understand and experience its existence. The only way we can access the story is by moving from word to word in the hope that it will appear within us. Henri Bortoft reflects on this dynamic between the part and whole in his 1971 journal paper on *Counterfeit and Authentic Wholes*. He affirms:

> The whole is nowhere to be encountered except in the midst of the parts. It is not to be encountered by stepping back to take an overview, for it is not over and above the parts, as if it were some superior over-arching part. The whole is to be encountered by stepping right into the parts.[5]

Let us practically discover the experience of moving from part to part to 'understand' something smaller than a whole story. Use the exercise below to explore your *experience* of understanding a sentence and to notice whether the process of understanding unfolds within you, during either of the steps. Go slowly so that you can pay attention to noticing your experience as it is happening.

EXERCISE: THE WHOLE AND THE PARTS

1. Read each word below as slowly as you can and intentionally pause between each word. Sound the words out separately in your mind and focus your attention on the experience of saying each word individually.

    I each the a eventually hope emerge time sentence

    meaning one that at in am the reading of may word the

2. Next, read the same words arranged in the sentence below.
    Read them once slowly, and then, read the sentence again
    several times at your usual reading speed. Pay attention
    to the way in which you experience your understanding
    emerging as you move from word to word.

I am reading each word, one at a time, in the hope that

the meaning of the sentence may eventually emerge.

Reflection: Use your imagination to compare the two
experiences. How did your experience of reading the list
of words compare with reading them in a sentence? When
reading the words as a coherent, whole sentence were you
able to notice the way in which the meaning of the sentence
emerged as you were reading? How is the meaning of the
whole sentence different from the meaning of the individual
words themselves?

In order to 'read' a sentence we simultaneously observe the individual
words with our eyes in a linear, methodical fashion but the process of
understanding itself is non-linear. As we begin to read the individual
words of a sentence, one by one, each word helps to bring forth the
meaning of the *whole* sentence. However, the meaning of the words we
have already read is also directly influenced by the words that are yet to
come, *and* the meaning of each word is also further determined by the
meaning of the sentence as a whole. So, the wholeness (or meaning)
of a sentence is dependent on the parts to come into being, but for
the parts to really mean anything (and thus also, to fully come into
being) they are dependent on the sentence as a whole. This non-linear
interaction between parts and wholes demonstrates the dynamic
way in which wholeness is expressed, and the way in which it can be
understood; to understand the whole, or wholeness, of a sentence (or
any part of life) we must first enter into its parts. Following the work
of Henri Bortoft[6], we will now explore the metaphor of a hologram
as a way of further investigating the nature of wholeness, and the
dynamics and attributes of authentic wholes.[7]

A hologram of Princess Leia

A hologram is created by projecting the light of a laser onto a holographic plate; the result is a 3D representation of an image. A well-known example of this is the holographic projection of Princess Leia in the blockbuster movie *Star Wars*. If we were to remove part of Princess Leia's holographic plate, for example, let's say we broke the top-right corner off, the projected 3D image of her would remain whole. If we kept removing parts of the plate, reducing its overall size, the resolution of the hologram would lessen and her image would fade. However, as long as at least part of the plate remained, the image of Princess Leia would still remain whole. In a hologram, the whole image is present in every part of a holographic plate, therefore the wholeness of the image is irreducible. In contrast, if we had a printed poster of Princess Leia and started tearing off sections of the poster, the 'whole' image would immediately begin to disappear. The more of the poster that we removed, the less 'whole' the image would become and we would end up with only a handful of fragments, none of which would contain the whole image of Princess Leia.

The 'whole' that is presented in the example of the poster represents our common understanding of wholes as finite, solid objects – as soon as we remove a part the whole becomes incomplete. In contrast, the 'whole', which is presented in the example of the hologram, which Henri calls an 'authentic' whole, reflects the type of wholes that nature creates, where the whole is always present in the parts. This type of organic, or holographic, whole cannot be reduced by simply removing 'parts' of it. As with the holographic plate, the wholeness of nature is irreducible, it is a concealed potential that is ever-present as long as a 'part' of it remains. For instance, the wholeness of an apple tree still remains even if you cut off one, or all, of its branches. The remaining parts still contain its essential nature and will continue to express that wholeness in any way they can, such as sprouting new branches from its trunk. Henri Bortoft describes the paradoxical dynamic between an authentic whole and its parts in his 1971 journal paper on wholeness:

> The essential irreducibility of the whole is such that it would seem inconceivable at first that there could be any sense in which the whole could be said to have parts. This inconceivability arises in some degree from the strength of the statement that the whole is whole; but it also arises from an unnoticed preconception of the relation between parts and whole, a preconception which is such as to deny effectively the primacy of the whole.[8]

For us to begin to wrap our minds around the way in which nature creates organic 'wholes' it is also important to explore the ways in which we think that 'wholes' are created. One common understanding is that a 'whole' is created as a result of an integration of parts. This implies a linear sequence of events that leads up to the creation of *the* whole, as though the whole were an entire object. This way of thinking about creating 'wholes' requires the parts to be present first, so that they can be slotted together in order to make up the totality of the whole, similar to the way in which a jigsaw puzzle or Lego set is assembled. In this case, the whole is not 'whole' until the last part has been slotted into place.

Another common understanding of how a 'whole' is created assumes the reverse of this linear sequence – that a whole must be present before the parts so that the whole can determine what those parts are and how they function. This is often the case in mainstream organisations such as corporations. In order to create the whole (corporation) a multitude of specialised, individual parts (jobs) are created, such as cleaners, manual workers, administrators, accountants, managers and directors, all of whom are assigned separate cubicles, offices or floors, and given specific tasks to carry out, which are determined by, and in service of, the whole (corporation).

In the first example of creating 'wholes', such as we find with jigsaw puzzles or sets of Lego, it is the parts which create the whole, and so the whole is dependent on the parts. In fact, this whole form is not really a 'whole' as such, it is a collection of independent parts which, when combined, express the idea of a physical whole. In the second example, the 'whole' corporation itself creates the parts, or jobs, therefore the parts are dependent on the whole. In this case, rather than being whole, the corporation is actually a kind of 'super part' which dominates the parts that it creates by sitting over and above them, assuming significance, supremacy, and superiority.

Both of these examples of 'wholes' are what Henri Bortoft called 'counterfeit' wholes, defined as such because they are each made up of inauthentic relationships. They both consist of a collection of separate parts that have been assembled, in a linear way, in order to create the 'whole', either in a bottom-up or a top-down direction. There are no intrinsic connections *between* the parts; they have just been put together.

By contrast, 'authentic' wholes – the organic wholes that we find in nature, such as micro-organisms, plants, animals, whole ecosystems and so on – are created by an ongoing, interactive 'dialogue' between the parts and the whole(s) of which they are a part. Unlike counterfeit wholes, which operate as separate entities, authentic wholes are nested inside one and other. For example, a whole cell is a part of a whole organ, which is a part of a whole body, and the whole body is part of a whole eco-system, which is part of the whole planet, and the whole planet is part of a whole solar system, and so on.

An authentic whole is not a form as such, but more of a coherent integrity which becomes expressed through the parts that make up its form. As Henri used to say, in regards to authentic wholes, the parts are a place for the 'presencing' of the whole. These 'parts' are not owned or determined by the whole but the whole *does* provide the coherence around which its parts can form. The parts themselves rely on the coherent integrity of the whole to *guide* their development, but they are not slaves to the whole. For example, as we saw above, an apple tree is an authentic whole. Its wholeness, or 'appleness', is what it means-to-be an apple tree, its characteristic nature. This essential nature is *expressed* through an apple tree's leaves, branches, fruit, seeds and so on, but these parts of the apple tree are not *determined* by the whole, as though they already existed as exact images, in blueprint form, before the parts came into being. Instead, each part, such as a particular apple that is growing on a tree, has a degree of freedom, plasticity and autonomy within the way in which it is able to create its form. However, there are still boundaries and limits, for example, the individual branches on one apple tree will *all* be slightly different, but a branch of an apple tree cannot just spontaneously turn into the branch of orange tree of its own accord.

In an authentic whole there is an intrinsic *relationship* between the parts and the whole but neither the part nor whole is dominant; they are not separate entities and cannot be separated. The whole cannot exist without the parts and the parts cannot exist without the whole, therefore, as they each rely on the other to come into being, the parts and the whole are equally interdependent, and have a mutual interest in maintaining the coherence and integrity of the whole.

Counterfeit stock cubes

Our ability to perceive wholeness, and to distinguish between authentic and counterfeit wholes, can help us to recognise what is genuine, and most satisfying, in our everyday lives. Wholeness, which is expressed by authentic wholes, embodies meaning and integrity. In response to a questionnaire that I developed as part of my MSc dissertation research, Henri Bortoft commented that, 'Whenever there is an experience of wholeness the experience is *ipso facto* meaningful – and very satisfying'.[9] As wholeness is inherently meaningful and satisfying, if we consume something without wholeness it usually leaves us feeling either physically or psychologically dissatisfied. This is often the case for many of the mass-produced goods and services that are available today.

In our modern world, the wholeness or essential nature of everyday products, such as processed food items, has been steadily undermined by the legal obligation of companies to maximise profits. For instance, there is a well-known brand of stock cube that my mother used to buy when I was growing up that we used to assist the gravy-making process for our Sunday dinners. At that time this stock cube was made entirely of concentrated beef stock. We recently checked the packaging whilst on a curious trip around a supermarket only to find that these stock cubes now contain no beef stock at all, only artificial colourings, flavourings and chemical flavour enhancers such as monosodium glutamate. This product, like many others on our supermarket shelves, is presenting an *idea* of a whole product, but it is in fact a counterfeit whole. Since the stock cube has lost its integrity, and its wholeness, what started out as a helpful addition to our store cupboard has now been turned into something that is nutritionally dissatisfying and could even potentially be damaging to our health.

In addition to the brands who have turned their once genuine products into counterfeit versions of themselves, there has also been an explosion of fake goods around the world in recent years. Luxury brand handbags are routinely copied and sold on the black market. These 'copies' are sold as reflections of a 'whole' product but they are not *genuine*, they lack the quality and integrity of the original, such as fine craftsmanship, authentic materials and attention to detail. Even more worryingly, in China there have been cases of fake soy sauce made partially from human hair, not to mention fake eggs, and fake baby milk.

The rise of fake products and the increasing decline in the quality of goods from brands that many people used to love and trust, both of which sell an 'idea' rather than provide the genuine article, still demonstrates the authentic, dynamic nature of wholeness even though the individual products represent counterfeit wholes. This is due to the way in which these goods are themselves products of the larger wholes of which they are a part, such as the economy. The purpose of a whole *is* its coherent integrity, but when that purpose is designed purely for self-interest, which in this case is the interest of the economy itself, there is no space for relationships or dialogue to emerge *between* the whole and its parts. Therefore, as the 'whole' economy is centred around self-interest, if the parts of the economy wish to survive, they must either find a way to subsist independently of the whole, or become subservient (slaves) to it.

The economy, as a whole, creates and takes on 'parts' for no other reason than to maintain and serve itself. This nature of our economy, which is quite literally 'self-centred', leads its dependent parts – people – to search for ways in which to fulfil the purpose of the whole out of necessity and a matter of survival, rather than out of genuine support and cooperation. Contrary to the way in which they are marketed, goods such as 'counterfeit' stock cubes are designed, developed and manufactured by individual people (the constituent parts of the economic system) in order to fulfil the purpose of the whole brand, the whole business and the whole economy of which they are a part – and this purpose is to continually make, and to exponentially increase, profit.

In nature 'wholes', such as plants, insects, rocks, and animals, are created by a series of interconnected, complex processes and relationships which allows physical form to emerge in dialogue *with* its immediate surroundings, and the result is that these parts of nature usually integrate themselves seamlessly into the whole eco-system, or the particular environment, of which they are a part. For example, in order for an apple tree to create and maintain its physical form the tree uses resources from the local soil and atmosphere that it is growing in. However, the parts which it then discards either contribute towards creating new life, such as seeds, or help to sustain existing life, such as the fallen leaves that nourish bacteria and fungi on the ground. That is not to say that self-interest does not exist in nature, it does. A single population can grow in size for as long it can sustain its needs for subsistence but the unchecked growth of a plant or animal species can lead the organisms to literally eat themselves out of house and home. In nature, unchecked self-interest ultimately ends in extinction.

Many people speak about how individuals today are 'separated' or 'disconnected' from nature but this is not wholly true. It is physically impossible to separate ourselves from the air we breathe or the food and water that sustain us. The crisis lies within our perception – a way of seeing that 'sees' separation. The neo-liberal economy is just one example of the way in which we have created, and idolised, a form of life which mirrors our own way of seeing 'separation'. As individuals, if we do not develop a dynamic way of seeing we will not be able to notice the dynamic, relational dimensions of life to their full extent and overcome this perception of separation.

For many people nature is like a book written in a foreign language, it is seen to exist but remains largely meaningless. We can remedy this. By exploring the ways in which we see the world, we can get to know life, and nature, in terms of itself. Only once we have recognised, and made an effort to move beyond, our own limited ways of perceiving the world can we open ourselves up to seeing and understanding the ways in which life can create and maintain itself, with freedom, creativity, integrity and autonomy, yet still remain in harmony as a whole.

In nature, in order for a whole to thrive, its parts must thrive also. The same goes for societies, neither the part nor the whole can dominate, they need to authentically work together. As individuals, by endeavouring to understand what it means *to be* a part of an authentic whole we can then begin to co-create our own whole communities, societies and systems that will allow people and the planet to thrive.

Part Two: Giving Life Our Full Attention

5. A Fresh Approach to Life

All is suddenly suffused with meaning. Once this leap has been made, once wonder and awakening have flashed upon us, we inevitably fall back into our half-sleep – but with a difference, for a radical change in perception and feeling has taken place.

Frederick Franck. The Zen of Seeing[1]

Feeling wonder

A few years ago I was fortunate enough to have skiing lessons on some Italian ski slopes that cover the underside of the Matterhorn, a mountain in the Alps which sits on the border between Italy and Switzerland. On one particular day I remember sitting alone, high up on a snowy plateau, taking a breather. It was late afternoon but the sky was still bright blue and sunny. Leaning my hands and body on the snow I rested for awhile and immersed my senses in the icy landscape. As I scanned the slopes with my eyes I felt the frosty air gently biting at my cheeks. In the distance I observed long slithers of blue-grey shadows stretching slowly down the sides of the mountains and noticed, on the rest of the landscape, that the fading sunlight set off a lively sparkle in every ice crystal that it touched. This soft showering of late afternoon light made the silent winter landscape glisten and come to life. The scene was so breathtakingly beautiful that I was struck still by it, fixed to the ground with awe and wonder.

It was immensely satisfying to feel wonder wash over me that day. My whole body felt as though it were smiling but not just from simple pleasure, it felt deeper than that. It was as though the wintry mountain scene had reached deep inside me and had opened up every last part of my body, from the top of my head to the tips of my toes.

The experience of wonder had called my whole being to attention, softening my body, my heart and my mind, yet sharpening my awareness. I was fully immersed in my experience, my senses enlivened and drawn outwards toward the magnificence of the landscape, yet I also felt inwardly expanded, touched by something far bigger than the small part of the world that I could actually see with my eyes.

For me, it is experiences of wonder like this that makes life worth living, these experiences change my relationship to life and make me value and appreciate life more. The mystery and magnificence of wonder, which momentarily draws me out of myself and away from all I think I know, is both humbling and exciting. Of course, this type of experience emerges most effortlessly when we have an obviously wondrous scene laid out before us. Sweeping panoramic views from high up in the Alps or jaw-dropping urban views from the top of teetering high buildings, such as the Shard in London, or the Empire State Building in New York, require little or no effort to take our breath away. These experiences also breathe a different kind of sustenance back into us; they inspire us and somehow seem to usher life directly inside us.

Unfortunately our daily lives tend not to induce such awe-inspiring feelings so effortlessly. As we gradually settle in to a new job, a new house, a new romantic partnership or a new town, our daily lives soon become filled with ordinariness. This can often be the source of much discontent as the experiences we have with parts of life that we perceive to be 'ordinary' often feel dull and unexciting, lacking in life. We therefore tend to approach these ordinary aspects of life with feelings of boredom or even contempt. To combat the ordinariness of our daily lives we often try to escape them, either physically or mentally, in order to give ourselves experiences that have the enlivening effect which wonder brings. These escapes might include flying overseas to holiday in 'exotic' destinations; searching the internet or shopping malls for the next must-have gadget, smartphone, or pair of shoes; or spending time fantasising about our dream house, job or partner and the perfect life that would accompany them. However, once our holidays, shopping trips and fantasies are over, we find that our routine, mundane lives are still right where we left them.

The label of ordinariness that our everyday perception slaps bountifully on anything in life that has come to be familiar, is like a kiss of death and leads us to take everything that it touches for granted. The more familiar a part of life becomes to us, the less we really *see* it, and therefore, the less we are in awe of it. As our sense of wonder fades yesterday's 'must-have' smartphone or pair of shoes soon becomes old news and we begin to find less satisfaction in our 'ideal job' or even in our 'perfect partner'. Even if we do manage to buy all the phones and shoes that we have dreamed of, or enter into relations with the people we are in awe of, unless we notice the habit that our everyday perception has of leaving us blind to life, the novelty will keep wearing off, we will keep getting bored, and our relationships to those possessions and people will suffer.

Seeing with fresh new eyes

As we explored in Chapter 1, allowing our attention to be distracted by our definitions and organising ideas limits the way in which we can see life. When we become aware of these automatic suggestions that our minds present us with we can choose to temporarily put them to one side and concentrate our efforts on seeing the world with 'fresh new eyes'. This process of monitoring and refreshing our perception can improve the way we relate to everything that we encounter everyday. One way of revitalising our perception of everyday life is by actively challenging our mind's suggestions that daily life is boring and mundane. For instance, if we see the town that we live in through 'eyes' that think they know it inside and out, and automatically expect to see nothing different, then we are unlikely to feel any wonder or to notice anything different. The same goes for our partner, our parents, our work colleagues and our friends; we will not *see* anything 'new' until we expect something new to be seen.

By making an effort to see life with fresh new eyes, as though we were meeting it for the first time, we can expect there to be mystery and hold a possibility for the unexpected to emerge. This fresh approach to experiencing life can enliven both us and our perception of the world around us. As the artist Frederick Franck wrote:

> Everyone thinks he knows what a lettuce looks like. But
> start to draw one and you realise the anomaly of having

lived with lettuces all your life but never having seen one
...What applies to lettuces, applies equally to the all-too-
familiar faces of husbands... wives...[2]

Fortunately, we do not need to stand on a mountaintop everyday to bring wonder into our daily lives. However, if we want to perceive wonder in something that our mind has already defined as ordinary, or familiar, seeing it with fresh new eyes does require a conscious effort, yet from this effort a deeper respect, gratitude and reverence for life can emerge. For example, when I see my mother, I *know* that she is my mother. There is a quality to our relationship that is eternal and unchanging. She is and always will be my mother, that is a fact. Even when her physical presence is no longer here, the fact that she gave birth to me will remain a certainty in the fabric of time. Yet my mother is actually a 'different' person each time that I meet her as, like every other human being on the planet, my mother's physicality, moods, thoughts and feelings change and evolve every second of every day. Therefore, there will *always* be more to her than meets the eye and, in terms of my experience of her, there will always be more to her than is already in my mind.

My own organising idea of my 'mother' presences a universal quality of her being which is timeless and unchanging, but understanding that she is also different every time that I meet her allows me to open my mind to noticing new things about her and it gives her the space to become more than I already think she is. Paying full attention to my experience of my mother, as she is, beyond my pre-existing ideas about her, helps me to not take her for granted and to be increasingly grateful for the time that we do get to spend together. As Goethe said, 'The hardest thing to see is what is in front of your eyes'. This is especially true with our loved ones but applies equally to everything that we encounter in life, be it our smartphones, shoes, towns and cities, or the planet we live on.

Once we become familiar with any person in our life, whether it is a partner, friend or colleague, we often stop being curious and stop relating to them in the present moment. Instead we respond to them as if we are speaking to past versions of themselves. We remember things that they have already said or done on past occasions, and then expect them to think, do or feel something similar this time.

This can be especially damaging for our personal lives as it leads us to make mindless assumptions that slowly but surely squeeze the life out of even our most intimate relationships. In his book *Curious?* Todd Kashdan reports that, from his research and practice as a clinical psychologist, he has found that curiosity and openness are the key to maintaining satisfying relationships:

> One of the top reasons that couples seek counseling or
> therapy is pure boredom. This is often the starting point
> of resentment, hostility, communication breakdowns, and
> a lack of interest in spending time together ... Curious
> people report more satisfying relationships and marriages.
> Happy couples describe their partners as interested and
> responsive.[3]

As we habitually tend to overemphasise what we *expect* to see in our everyday lives, we are rarely aware of the full capabilities of the people and parts of life that are closest to us. These expectations lead to a perceptual blindness, or blind spots, which either underemphasise or completely fail to recognise the aspects of life which we hadn't expected to see. Instead of presuming that we 'know' those closest to us, we can overcome these limitations by being *curious* when we interact with them.

For example, we can explore what it feels like to be on the receiving end of curiosity by bringing to mind a past experience of someone giving *us* their full attention. If the curious attention was delivered with care, it is likely that the way in which they listened, and gave their attention, made us feel valued and worthy of respect. This sits in stark contrast to the frustration that we feel when it is obvious that people are not giving us their full attention or showing an interest in what we are saying. When we focus our undivided attention on another person in a sensitive, curious, and open-minded way, it can be a great gift, enabling that person to feel actively seen and heard.

As I found with the way in which I perceive my mother, when we appreciate the people we encounter in our everyday lives with curiosity, and fresh new eyes, then we often begin to value them more. This can increase the degree of gratitude we feel as a result of having them in our lives. In the case of a romantic relationship, it can also increase how attracted we are to that person. Esther Perel, the author of *Mating in Captivity* believes that: 'Love rests on two pillars: surrender and autonomy. Our need for togetherness exists alongside our need for separateness.'[4] We can assist our partner's sense of autonomy, or need for separateness, by leaning back from our own familiar way of seeing them. By giving our partner the space to follow their own interests and passions we can find new ways to experience them, as when we observe them in new situations we give ourselves the chance to learn new things about them. Giving our partner the freedom to meet with new friends and try out new activities will draw out parts of them that we may have never seen before. Through curiously beholding the other person as they engage in new experiences we can enjoy realising that there are always unknown aspects of our partner that are yet to be discovered.

Curiosity is a powerful tool for bringing life to the world. Aside from altering how we experience the life in the present moment, enlivening our relationships and providing fuel to sustain our practice of giving life our full attention, current scientific research is now finding that the effect of practising curiosity also has significant health implications that influence how long we live and how healthy our minds are in later life. In *Curious?* Todd Kashdan writes:

> More than 2,000 older adults aged 60 to 86 were carefully observed over a five-year period and those who were more curious at the beginning of the study were more likely to be alive at the end of the study, even after taking into account age, whether they smoked, the presence of cancer or cardiovascular disease ...[5]

The enlivening benefits of curiosity are also mentioned in the book *Brain Rules*, which summarises what scientists currently know for sure about the ways in which our brains work. The author John Medina affirms that his most important brain rule is curiosity. His review of current neuroscience shows that our brains are wired to keep learning as we age and that the areas of the brain that are responsible for learning actually remain as malleable in our adult years as they were when we were a baby. In the book John illustrates the link between curiosity, a long life and a healthy mind with a story about his experience of the Nobel prize-winning scientists Edmund Fischer and Edwin Krebs. When he met them they were already in their mid-seventies and still working in a university. He described them as, '... creative as artists, wise as Solomon, lively as children. They had lost *nothing*. Their intellectual engines were still revving, and curiosity remained the fuel'.[6] Both these examples of research show that curiosity not only brings the world that we perceive to life, but as individuals, it can also help to keep us alive and full of life.

Aside from its enlivening effect, the physicist Albert Einstein provides a perfect example of the creativity and innovation that a curious mind can bring forth. As Todd Kashdan writes in *Curious?*:

> When asked about his uniqueness, Albert Einstein ... claimed that that his accomplishments had to do with an appreciation of the little mysteries of everyday life that others often take for granted ... His drive to search, ask questions, and explore the vast unknown was as important to him as the drive to find answers. It is an approach to living that is simple to understand and rare in practice.[7]

Living context

As the American writer Henry Miller is frequently quoted as saying, 'The moment one gives close attention to anything, even a blade of grass, it becomes a mysterious, awesome, indescribably magnificent world in itself.' Being able to experience the most ordinary parts of life with fresh new eyes and with curiosity, whether it is our coffee mug or tea pot, our car or our bicycle, our back garden or our local park, can seem impossible at first, but if we spend a moment contemplating their living context it can help to shine a light on quite how amazing they actually are.

We can do this by what I call 'unpacking' the living context of life. This involves imaginatively exploring the processes of where, how, from what and from whom a part of life came. Using our imagination to bring to life the living context of an object, a person, or even an idea, does not mean that we create a fantasy about that part of life but use our individual and collective experience, and pre-existing knowledge, to bring its life story alive in our mind. Let's try this with an everyday coffee mug.

To look at *who* our coffee mug came from we can try to imagine and visualise the many hands that the mug has passed through before it found its way into ours, such as shop assistants, shelf stackers, craftsmen or factory workers. To consider *what* our mug came from we can think about its physical aspects, such as the raw materials that were dug from the earth in order to make our coffee mug, the glaze which was used to finish it, or the paint that was used to decorate it. To explore *how* our mug came into being we can contemplate the processes needed to craft it into its finished form, such as a piece of clay that is worked into a specific shape by hand, then glazed and fired, or a ceramic mixture that is mechanically poured into a mould on a factory line. Reflecting on *where* our coffee mug came from involves thinking about the shop that we bought it in, the distance and places that the mug might have travelled in order to reach the shop, and the place that the coffee mug was originally created in, such as factory or a workshop. By bringing to mind the 'life' of these processes that were necessary in order for our coffee mug to come into being we can become aware of its life history and living context.

Perhaps most importantly for evoking wonder, we can also imaginatively explore *where* our everyday coffee mug is from within a planetary and astronomical context – the mug itself exists on exactly the same planet as us, and is made from atoms that at some point in the very, very distant past were stardust, just as our atoms were. Wow, our everyday coffee mug *is* pretty amazing.

At first glance this exercise may appear to be more suited to children than adults but, as Albert Einstein showed, exploring the 'little mysteries of everyday life' that we would otherwise take for granted, whether it is objects, people, places and or ideas, makes it possible for us expand our understanding of them.

Everything around us is imbued with the deep mystery and beauty of the unknown whether we pay attention to it or not. Understanding the context in which a part of life emerges can help to spark a sense of wonder within us. Let us use our imaginations to stop and very simply consider our own living context for a moment. Our birthplace is not just the town or city that we were born in, it is on a giant ball of rock, fire and water that we depend on to survive, from the minute we were born, to the day that we die. This gigantic ball of rock that we call Planet Earth is circling around a much, much larger ball of fire that we call the 'sun', which both the Earth and ourselves depend on for survival. Human beings are minute in comparison to these gigantic spheres, yet along with the sun and the earth, we all exist within an almost incomprehensible vastness, a mind-boggling emptiness, that we call 'space'. *This* is our everyday existence. This is the living context and the reality of our everyday lives, and it is amazing. However, if we get caught up in the illusion of familiarity and do not occasionally stop to consider quite how miraculous and wondrous our existence really is, our everyday lives might never feel very remarkable.

Love and knowledge

Using our full attention to notice our experience of life in the present moment and, at least temporarily, unconditionally accept what we find, makes it possible for us to open ourselves to the opportunity of knowing something *as it is* and in terms of itself. As we explored together in Part One, this process of living attentively enables us to notice details in life that we usually don't notice, including our own habits of mind. The action of devoting our attention to noticing the world in such an intimate and uncensored way is like choosing to love, or to fall in love with, everything that we meet and creates the conditions for a type of knowledge to emerge that is akin to love itself. Not a romantic, physical kind of love, such as Éros, but a form of love which is closer to the selfless love that the Greeks describe as Agápe. This is the love of seeing and unconditionally accepting what it is, *as it is*.

Falling in love today commonly signifies an intimate, romantic connection or relationship, that is cultivated with one 'significant' other. This 'one' big relationship usually has a lot of emphasis put on it, both by our modern culture, and the couple themselves. Once we have a 'significant' other, we often then save certain ways of being exclusively for that one relationship, such as intimacy, sensitivity, vulnerability, and their associated skills which include empathy, deep listening, care and affection. It is socially acceptable in modern western culture to display these qualities to a partner, to our closest friends or to family members, where they are considered strengths, but these so called 'soft skills' are often deemed unnecessary or irrelevant when we are building businesses, conducting research, designing systems or developing 'knowledge'. Therefore, we are often not encouraged to actively employ them when carrying out studies or projects in our classrooms, offices or research labs.

At one time I also went along with this line of thought, until I was introduced to a method of inquiry that uses these 'soft skills' as part of a practice which strives to understand life in terms of itself. This practice, and academic discipline, that I am very passionate about, is called phenomenology; for me it demonstrates the point at which love becomes knowledge and knowledge becomes love.

I was first introduced to phenomenology when I was studying with Henri Bortoft. I still remember that at the time the term 'phenomenology' felt very alien to me and conjured up images of an elusive academic enigma that I would never be able to fully get to grips with, and I have since found that the word often becomes an instant barrier to many people that I meet. This is not surprising as the word rarely trips smoothly off the tongue and either tends to play on people's academic insecurities, or just sounds incredibly complicated or mysterious. When I am teaching, especially in non-formal education, I often choose to avoid the word altogether. Instead, I prefer to lead people straight into practising phenomenology so that they have a chance to *experience* it before their minds put them off.

I have applied the same approach with this book. In the first half of the book we explored a series of stepping stones designed to reflect the stages involved when carrying out a phenomenological inquiry. These stages include setting aside preconceptions, assumptions, definitions and judgements; seeking to explore the phenomenon in an empathic way in order to get to know it in terms of itself; describing, critically yet fairly, the way in which we experience the phenomenon, as if it could speak itself; and finally reflecting on our experiences to search for intrinsic patterns, qualities, relationships that *belong* to the phenomenon itself and, with them, an understanding of its essential nature, or wholeness.

Now that we have progressed through Part One, and have lived experience of practising phenomenology, in order to shed further light on how this book came into being, I will share a little of its living context.

Phenomenology is an expression of a dynamic way of seeing in action, and has manifested as a well-respected philosophy, a rigorous academic discipline and a widely practised research methodology. However, what I feel is most important with regards to the ways in which I personally use it, and the potential benefits that it can bring to humanity in general, is that it is fundamentally a *way of being* in, and relating to, life. Phenomenology is a gently disciplined approach to a certain way of being human that allows life to thrive, both inside and outside of us. It accomplishes this enlivening effect by striving to see the world in terms of itself and on its own terms. To do this, phenomenological practice uses what Goethe called 'a delicate empiricism'. This is a delicate yet full attention that is utterly focused on our experience of life, and in doing so, creates the conditions for the phenomenon itself to become its own theory through our direct experience of it.

Phenomenology arose within western philosophy from a group of continental philosophers at the beginning of the twentieth century. Starting in the early 1900s with Edmund Husserl, continuing throughout the century with Martin Heidegger and later Maurice Merleau-Ponty. Although it was originally developed from philosophical inquiry, during the twenty-first century phenomenology has developed into a qualitative research methodology that is currently practised all over the world and used in many disciplines, such as psychology, medicine and the social sciences.

The practice of phenomenology acknowledges that within our direct experience there is a connection created *between* us and the world, and through this union we can perceive truths that are not just an accurate reflection of our own individual experience, but that are true to the world itself. This form of 'knowing', or knowledge gathering, is called intersubjectivity. As it explicitly acknowledges a connection between the 'knower' and the part of life becoming known, phenomenological inquiry transcends the dualism of objectivity and subjectivity, which features so prominently in our educational, academic and scientific institutions today. Objectivity involves believing that you can separate intellectual knowledge from other aspects of our human experience such as our emotions, personal biases and sensory experience. On the other hand, subjectivity involves believing that the 'truth' of our experience belongs only to us as an individual and that it is not an accurate representation of a 'truth' in the world.

The dualism of subjectivity and objectivity is actually only perceptible by the rational mind itself – the brain's 'left-hemisphere' way of seeing – which separates knowledge from experience in order to categorise and define it. The duality may feel true to this part of our mind but it is not consistent with our experience. Our bodies, minds, thoughts and feelings are not located separately inside us, each in its own neat little box, and we do not have an internal switch that can turn subjectivity 'off' and turn objectivity 'on'. As phenomenology is grounded in experience, not in theory, it is aware that there is no such thing as absolute objectivity. In this way the practice of phenomenology radically and honestly confronts the paradox of what it means to be human – that we have individual autonomy and free will, and yet are also inextricably intertwined with everything that we experience. As my former teacher, the biologist Brian Goodwin, wrote in his captivating book *Nature's Due: Healing Our Fragmented Culture*:

> The result is a sympathetic union of the knower and the
> known without losing their distinctness. The process of
> knowing through participation is driven by love and trust
> of the real.[8]

Phenomenology is also an embodied practice, in the sense that it gives attention to our entire spectrum of human experience, including our sensing bodies. Unlike other research methodologies, our physical bodies, feelings, intuition and sense experience do not need to be disregarded and put at the bottom of the pile in order to give precedence to hypothesising, theorising, defining and intellectualising our experience.

The key to phenomenology is that it strives to notice, and make visible, the parts of life that usually remain unnoticed, yet, most importantly, it notices without attachment. This does not mean that phenomenological inquiry considers itself above and beyond the phenomenon being studied, on the contrary, it makes a conscious effort to become as invisible as possible so that the part of life being studied can reveal itself on its own terms. By paying careful attention to discerning the difference between thoughts, ideas or feelings that we project onto the world, and our direct experience of the world itself, phenomenology exercises a type of thinking that is both critical and fair. This way of thinking explicitly acknowledges that it is directly connected to the world yet leans back, or gives the world just enough space, to be able to see the part of life being studied *as it is*.

Although many academic phenomenologists might not admit it, the receptive way of being, unconditional acceptance, and gentle yet disciplined approach that phenomenology uses to relate to life cultivates *love*. Through striving to get to know something in terms of itself, the practice of phenomenology inherently has reverence for, and preserves the life of, our experience and in so doing, it respects the *life* of life itself. After facilitating a weeklong course, I was shocked by an act of courageous honesty when a well respected academic colleague of mine disclosed to me and the group of students that, 'at the end of the day, phenomenology is all about love'. This is echoed by another well respected academic, Arthur Zajonc. In one of the most profound academic papers I have ever read he writes that, 'learning to love, is also the task of learning to know in its fullest sense'.[9] He starts the paper by saying:

> When the German poet Goethe declared, 'In all things
> we learn only from those we love,' he was speaking
> directly to the profound connection between cognition
> and affection. We are especially open to and receptive
> towards one we love. We are more likely to remember
> the words of a beloved mentor and to ruminate on them
> long after they were spoken. Teachings go deep when
> carried into the human being by deep affection; they can
> change us, teach us even to see the world differently. I have
> grown increasingly convinced of the importance of the
> connection between cognition and affection, or to state
> it more clearly, the crucial relationship between love and
> knowledge.[10]

The idea of loving an unfamiliar world in order to get to know it can at first seem sentimental and naïve, especially to our analytical minds. We are so conditioned in the West to associate love with romance and sentimentality, that it can be hard to recognise openness, receptivity and acceptance as forms of love. It may well be too challenging at this stage for our minds to think of the unconditional acceptance and radical openness that a phenomenological method, or dynamic way of seeing, practises as love. However, when we start to *practise* being open and receptive, and begin to directly experience the process of getting to know life *as it is*, the connection between love and knowledge will become apparent. By fully opening our hearts and minds to living attentively, not only can we get to know life in terms of itself but we might also transform the way in which we understand and experience love.

6. Seeing Inside Ourselves

Owning our story can be hard but not nearly as difficult as spending our lives running from it. Embracing our vulnerabilities is risky but not nearly as dangerous as giving up on love and belonging and joy – the experiences that make us the most vulnerable. Only when we are brave enough to explore the darkness will we discover the infinite power of our light.

Brené Brown[1]

Life crisis in Hong Kong

When I was twenty-one, I moved from England to Hong Kong. Over a period of five years I worked for a number of different corporations in lingerie design and product development. On one level, both life and work in Hong Kong were exciting, fast and fun. I enjoyed many corporate and expatriate luxuries. I socialised with friends and colleagues in the newest and most fashionable places in the city, attending launch parties and fashion shows, and was paid to go shopping in high-end stores as part of my design research. In one role, aged only twenty-three, I dined in Michelin-starred restaurants, stayed in five star hotels when I travelled for business trips and frequently charged bottles of vintage champagne to my company credit card.

Having grown up on the outskirts of a quiet, small town in the English countryside, I very much enjoyed the novelty and decadence of life in a fast-paced metropolis for a while. Outside my work, Hong Kong and South East Asia were exciting areas for me to explore, geographically and culturally. At the weekends I would spend my days relaxing on one of the numerous beaches, sunbathing or practising water sports, and often took boat trips around the islands with large groups of other expatriates. When I wasn't spending time outdoors in nature, I would search for tiny, hidden local restaurants on a quest to find the best Cantonese dim-sum or the tastiest Malaysian Laksa noodles. These explorations of Hong Kong's culture and nature were key to what kept me there for five years, as on a deeper level I found my life and work in the city lonely and superficial.

In my design work, my creative capabilities were largely left unused. The buyers I worked with from retail chains all over the world did not want originality; they wanted a 'cookie cutter' formula that would maximise their company's possibility of making money. This would involve endlessly re-producing styles that had already sold well or being requested to essentially 'copy' the designs of more expensive brands.

The garments I designed were also constantly undermined by my company, and client's, bottom line of profit, which needed always to increase exponentially. The requirement to continually and exponentially increase profit meant that myself, friends and colleagues faced invariable demands to endlessly meet higher targets and increased sales projections, orders and revenue. These demands created high-pressure environments in the work place and the resulting stress was generally offset by indulgence through expensive meals, exotic holidays, costly bar tabs or lavish shopping trips.

The most common way for expatriates to let off steam in Hong Kong was to party, hard and often. The majority of my social encounters at weekends revolved around drinking alcohol in bars and clubs with friends, often until the early hours of the morning. Working hard and playing hard in a city that felt as though it had no limits made my life feel surreal, as though I was in a playground for adults caught up in an Alice in Wonderland type of waking dream. The cocktail of extreme stress combined with the sensation of living in a fantasy pushed many corporate expatriates to seek solace in drugs, alcohol or sex, and led some to harmful, even fatal, addictions. Others, like myself, suffered from frequent bouts of depression and anxiety, and some even had their careers cut short by nervous breakdowns.

At the other end of the pay scale, the machinists who manufactured my designs in the factories that I visited were treated like robots. These men and women were only really there because we had not yet designed a machine that could take their place. They were given mindless tasks to repeat constantly for hours on end. The monotony and repetition of the work meant that these people were treated not as human beings but as just another cog in a giant economic machine. In some of the factories I worked in, the people sewing the garments were not even referred to by name but instead assigned a number. This particular quantification of their lives was just one example of the way in which these people were the casualties of a dominant way of thinking that had no capacity to comprehend their intrinsic value as people. This calculative view of life could only relate to them as commodities and recognise their value solely in regards to the financial cost of their labour. Unfortunately, in order for me and my colleagues to do our jobs 'well' we had to keep the 'value' of these people in the factories as low as possible in order to maximise the profit on the garments that we designed and they produced.

In Hong Kong, where I lived and worked, the city was always active twenty-four hours a day. Its streets would heave with people daily, rain or shine, yet these people rarely had time to stop and chat, or to take much notice of their surroundings. I had a few wonderful friends in the city but I still felt alone and extremely isolated, even though I was one in seven million. I would sit alone in my tiny, twenty-first floor apartment and imagine all of the people in all of the skyscrapers in Hong Kong as best I could. Then I would dissolve the walls of the buildings so that I could see the density of these people, so close in proximity, yet so separate from each other in their minds, hearts and lives. I felt the weight of this collective separation as if it had been placed directly onto my shoulders.

Each one of those seven million people was under pressure in some way *to become* the same 'individual' as everyone else, and to follow the rigid ideals that their family, colleagues, the media or society prescribed as benchmarks for social worth and acceptance, whether it was to become ever richer, thinner, prettier, sexier or more successful. These ideals were reinforced by row upon row of air-conditioned shopping malls which filled the dense urban spaces, touting a massive array of garments, products and gadgets. Gigantic billboards were plastered around the city, visually instructing women on how they 'should' look, which in Hong Kong is always thinner, with ever-whiter skin. These endless images that were attempting to sell abstracted ideals of 'perfection' suffocated the life out of me, along with many other people, by playing on our insecurities, creating feelings of never having enough, and induced the most destructive feeling of all – of never being good enough.

The whole city was set up to provide a relentless stream of 'ideals' for 'consumers' to purchase so that they could then strive to present those ideals themselves. The retailers and brands appeared to be more like drug dealers, providing the means for a manufactured social addiction. However, I eventually realised that it was all just a huge trick, a sleight of hand; the companies needed us in order to keep making a profit, they needed us to survive. They were not feeding us; we were feeding them. It was all a clever, painstakingly executed illusion. The big brands and corporations that dominated the city played on people's insecurities by manufacturing abstract, hollow ideals that were full of empty promises. Their imperative, and often sole purpose, was to make money and they did so by taking advantage of our basic human need for social acceptance.

Towards the end of the five years I gradually became more of a recluse as I retreated further into myself. Life became so overwhelming that eventually I was struggling to keep up with even the simplest tasks at work. Not only was I not happy but I also saw how unhappy people who worked as part of this economic machine seemed to be, whether it was my colleagues, our factory workers or the 'consumers' who bought the end products. At the same time, during my business travels through China I had noticed the extent to which the natural environment was being destroyed just to manufacture the garments that I was designing. Over five years I watched as the countryside lining the railway line from Shenzhen to Guangzhou in Southern China was steadily replaced with yet more homogenous grey factory buildings. An eruption of concrete spread along the land beside the railway lines like a rampant virus, consuming all the living natural resources it encountered and, like Medusa, this virus turned everything it touched into stone.

Taking my own personal unhappiness into account alongside the social exploitation and environmental destruction that I was witnessing my work began to feel ridiculously meaningless. I felt as though I was the only person in my personal and professional circles questioning the ideals and ways of living that we were being socially and economically pressured to uphold. If I tried to bring this into conversation with friends or colleagues I was often labelled as a dreamer or some kind of eccentric eco-warrior. I quickly became depressed and my sense of self-worth plummeted. Money did not make me happy, buying things did not make me happy and neither did success. I began to hate the way I looked and became very body conscious. Being a tall, young British woman amidst small, petite Asian girls, I quickly started to feel oversized and unattractive. This led to me date men with whom I was totally incompatible because I didn't believe that I deserved any better. I also started to become ill frequently. It felt as though something deep inside me couldn't cope anymore and began to shut down. I lost my spark, my *joie de vivre*.

I was re-presenting the ideal of the perfect twenty-first century young woman – intelligent, well-dressed, successful, well-travelled, and financially independent. However, inside I was slowly dying, embodying the words of the French philosopher Jean-Paul Sartre: 'Death draws the final point when we as beings cease to live for ourselves and permanently become objects that exist only for the outside world.'

The power of vulnerability

In retrospect, I now understand that no-one in Hong Kong had actually taken away my freedom or forced me to present myself in a certain way. I had eroded my own confidence and sense of self-worth by paying more attention to how people were seeing me than attending to my own well-being. I felt pressurised into presenting a version of myself that I thought the world would accept, rather than presencing what was authentically 'me'. This diversion of my attention towards other people's thoughts, labels and judgments prevented me from noticing what my needs were, so they were left unmet and consequently I suffered. I was sucked into the fallacy that popular ideas of how we *should* be, such as 'thinner' and 'prettier', are somehow more real and more important than our own individual experiences of life.

Even though it is so exhausting and damaging to present 'ideal' versions of ourselves, and deny our own truth, it is often easier than expressing our actual thoughts or feelings. Todd Kashdan is a clinical psychologist, professor of psychology and author of a number of books on subjects such as curiosity, happiness and social anxiety. He writes in his book *Curious?* that:

> Humans are creatures of habit, and it requires effort to be reflective and avoid labels ... the research is clear that the more we automatically and mindlessly categorize thoughts, feelings, and other people, the more we suffer. Well-being stumbles when we go on autopilot.[2]

Avoiding going on 'autopilot', and allowing the world to *see* us as we really are, often takes effort and courage, and it requires us to become vulnerable. Contrary to popular thought, vulnerability is a strength not a weakness, and it must be embraced as such if we wish to express ourselves authentically and stand up for what we believe in. Brené Brown is a writer, researcher, and educator from the US who studies authenticity, belonging and shame; she writes that: 'Vulnerability sounds like truth and feels like courage. Truth and courage aren't always comfortable, but they're never weakness'.[3] It wasn't until I found the courage to examine and embrace my own vulnerabilities, and my tendency to perceive myself as inadequate, that I could fully recognise the extent to which my mind's habit of defining life impacted the way I experienced myself every single day.

In a counselling session, four years after I had left Hong Kong, I had a metaphorical mirror held up to my face when the counsellor told me that by refusing to care and have kindness for myself, I was self-inflicting exactly the same kind of harm and violence that I was trying to fight against in the world. It was true. The belief that I wasn't 'good enough' had pervaded my being so deeply during my time in Hong Kong that even years later I was defining myself as unworthy of love, from myself and others. This led me to avoid situations in which I felt vulnerable and to hate myself so much that at times I even struggled to look at myself in the mirror. However, after this severe wake-up call, I realised that by refusing to be vulnerable, by being afraid to show my true self for fear of rejection, and by denying myself the same degree of care and attention that I was trying to give to the world, I was inhibiting the possibility of being an effective agent for change.

In the book *This is How: Surviving What You Think You Can't,* the author Augusten Burroughs writes that:

> The desire to impress somebody when you first meet them is caused by a tiny, invisible, freelance divorce attorney who sits on your shoulder and tells you what to do.[4]

This invisible voice tells us who we 'should' be and prevents us from being who we really are. Sharing our individual experiences of life with others makes us vulnerable, it opens us to criticism and judgment, yet shared experience is one of the most valuable and freely available assets that we have as human beings. The more we can trust the power of vulnerability, the more we can begin to share accounts of our individual experience as a force for good. Having the courage to share our real-life stories with others, rather than re-presenting an ideal, 'perfect' version of ourselves, enables us to transform the gaping holes that pain and misfortune have left inside us into gifts of experience.

Unconditional acceptance

Before we can authentically share our experience with others we need to first unconditionally accept ourselves, and what occurs inside us, without judgment. By temporarily suspending our opinions we can pay attention to noticing our thoughts, feelings, emotions and aspects of our behaviour, exactly as they are. Our insecurities and feelings of inadequacy usually lie beneath the surface of our everyday awareness, embedding themselves in familiar habits, but we need to connect to these insecurities, on their own terms, in order to really understand the current conditions of our inner world.

We most often present versions of ourselves when we are in the company of others and don't even necessarily realise we have shaped ourselves in some way to fit in with someone else's 'idea', of how or what we should be, until after it has happened. It is for this reason that some of our exploration has to be done on reflection. By digging beneath the surface of the ways in which we present ourselves, whether the aim is to be liked, accepted, or feel good enough, we can shine a light

119

underneath those re-presentations and examine the uncomfortable thoughts or feelings that are triggering this way of responding to life. Pema Chodron, a well-known female Western Buddhist teacher, teaches that once we have spent some time noticing when and how we are suffering we can bring our attention toward recognising what we have a 'propensity to get bothered by'.[5]

I remember being at a dinner party a few years ago with some acquaintances, all of whom were earning much more money than I was at the time and had had a much more expensive education. I sat at the table with my hands shaking as I struggled to appear confident and competent. My exact experience during that dinner was that I felt intimidated; not because of the ways in which the other guests were interacting with me, they were being friendly enough. The feeling of intimidation arose solely from comparing myself with them. Instead of unconditionally accepting myself I had measured myself against the few pieces of information that I had been given about them. My colleague Alex Balerdi, who is an integrative psychological therapist and mentor, always tells me that 'feelings follow actions'. In this instance the action of my mind was telling me that I was *not good enough* and my feelings, and physical reactions, followed. If, instead, I had acted with an attitude of unconditional acceptance, I would not have needed to concern myself with worrying about the life history of the other guests at the table. I could have then focused my full attention on just being myself and getting to know the people around the table, as they are, beyond my automatic definitions and judgments of them.

Buddhist scholar Pema Chodron refers to this process of complete acceptance as developing unconditional friendship with ourselves:

> Unconditional friendship means staying open when
> you want to shut down, when it is just too painful, too
> embarrassing, too unpleasant, too hateful what you see in
> yourself. The first step is looking at yourself with a feeling
> of gentleness and kindness.[6]

As Pema Chodron rightly states in her teachings, developing this basic friendship takes a lot of courage as our habitual responses tend to be harsh and critical, and often more so with ourselves. To develop unconditional friendship with ourselves we need to step away from our inner critic and instead adopt a more gentle approach. It can help to imagine how we would treat our own best friend if they were feeling exactly as we are. We would probably stick with them through all their ups and downs, fully accepting them and loving them no matter what. If we want to get to know ourselves beyond the habitual reactions and the representations that we project out into the world, this is the way in which we need to be treated too.

Intentionally adopting an attitude of unconditional acceptance can be used in this way, as a broad-focused tool, to become more alive during our interactions with others and to be kinder to ourselves. However, we can also use it in a more specific manner. Actively holding an attitude of unconditional acceptance enables us to intimately explore the depth and details of everything that we experience, inside and outside ourselves. Unconditionally accepting what it is, as it is, allows us to suspend our internal habits of mind that would otherwise try to fix or control what we see. In the case of our own true feelings, we often try to ignore them or squash them into some hidden corner of our being, but unconditionally accepting them allows us to really see them and get to know them as they are.

There is a popular trend in twenty-first century western culture that encourages us to control our feelings by forcing ourselves to be positive in order to 'move forward' and 'feel better' in our lives. However, unless we at least temporarily accept what is going on inside us we cannot identify exactly what it is that we are trying to hide or move away from. Misery does not leave us if we ignore what we are feeling and tell ourselves that we 'shouldn't' be miserable. Happiness does not usually increase just by telling ourselves that we 'should' be happy. Unconditionally accepting ourselves in our darkest moments, when we might feel ready to explode in violence, or even give up and die, may initially seem like defeat, as if we are giving in to our negativity. Or if we allow ourselves to really feel the intensity of our desire for cigarettes, chocolate or sex, it might seem like we are falling prey to our illicit urges. However, unconditionally accepting our feelings of desperation or our desire to smoke cigarettes allows us to get closer to them and explore these feelings. It allows us to notice our desires and urges without acting on them and to get to know them exactly as they are.

Pema Chodron calls this process 'feeling our feelings'.[7] By paying attention to the feeling of anger that arises when we feel offended we can put aside our thoughts about it being 'wrong' and concentrate on noticing, and really feeling, exactly what is being triggered inside us. If we feel we have been wronged, whether a friend insults us or a colleague undermines us, our bodies often experience some kind of discomfort. Tightness may occur in our throat or our stomach might start churning. Instead of launching straight into a knee-jerk reaction we can slow our perception down and turn our attention to what is happening inside us.

For example, instead of allowing ourselves to be distracted by the label 'anger' that our thoughts give to our feelings we can focus our attention fully on noticing the physical qualities we are experiencing, such as the dryness in our throat, the tightness in our jaw or the cramping sensation in our stomach. Pema Chodron has observed that by focusing our full attention on the feelings and accepting them without judgment, being with them, noticing them, and letting them flow, that this alone often has the effect of dissipating them. Our feelings have a finite life span. Each calls for our attention, and the more we push them away the deeper we bury them inside us, but if we accept them and give them our attention their grip on us lessens. Presencing our internal responses exactly as they are allows us to notice, to own and to take responsibility for our habitual reactions. By observing them over time, in relation to what we have a tendency to be triggered by, we can begin to identify what ignites our reactive emotional responses.

Being fully alive

I was fortunate enough to recently attend a lecture by Stephen Jenkinson, a Canadian teacher, author, and activist, who for a quarter of a century has been guiding individuals, couples, families and communities through all the human sufferings, sorrows and confusions concerning death. He has sat with over six hundred dying people during their moment of passing away and was the subject of a recent documentary film on death and dying called *Griefwalker*. In the lecture I attended, Stephen called our current civilisation the 'walking dead' and believes that the only way to remedy this is for each of us to muster the courage to become alive again by falling in love with life. He says that to do this we must have the courage to see life as it is, to bring our full attention to the coming and going of life, acknowledging that death and grief are intrinsic parts of it. To fall in love with life he believes that we need to hold an awareness of the inescapable death of everything that we encounter from the very beginning of our involvement with it, whether it be a child, a relationship, or a business that we have created. Every part of life that we engage with will cease to exist at some point. Death is the only certainty in life. Fully accepting this requires us to practise a kind of fearless love that acknowledges the end of all life but chooses to love anyway.

Holding the paradox of life and death together whilst we are in the middle of a relationship, a job or our own life is certainly not easy, but it also does not mean that we need to obsess over the unavoidable end of everything. When we fully acknowledge that whatever we are currently engaged in will end, sooner or later, the present moment suddenly becomes so much more precious and significant. By accepting that there is no 'forever', and no guarantee as to when the 'end' of anything will come, life becomes more immediate and we can become far more grateful for everything, and everyone, that we participate with.

All we can really be sure of in our everyday lives is a series of moments that are each 'now', and none of these moments come with a guarantee that there will be another quite like it, if any at all. For some the appearance of death is expected and welcomed, for others the sharp, unexpected disappearance of life is shocking and heart wrenching. Life can fall away from us as swiftly and abruptly as leaves falling from a tree, and there is no telling at which point we or our loved ones will join this inevitable descent.

When we accept that life does not keep going forever, the best we can do is to fully open our minds and our hearts to paying full attention to the life, and the people, that we are experiencing right now. This does not make those inevitable endings any less painful, on the contrary, the more we have opened and loved each moment of a person, a relationship or a particular time in our life, the stronger our pain and grief has probably been. However, if the grief is for a life well lived it does not live forever. It comes and goes, just as life itself.

For me, being aware that everything I am involved with will, at some point, end helps me to focus more intensely on the present moment, and the result is that I get a richer experience of life. This awareness also helps me bring acceptance, appreciation and gratitude to everything that I am doing, and makes it possible for me to genuinely love life more. After spending so much time at the bedside of dying people, Stephen Jenkinson considers the act of falling in love with life one of the biggest challenges that humans in the twenty-first century face, individually and collectively: 'Life does not give life. It's the end of life that gives life a chance. The world whispers, "all that we need of you is that you be human".'[8]

The wisdom of Stephen is also echoed in another great maestro of life, the world-renowned German conductor Karl Masur. The living vitality with which he enlivens the incredible musical compositions that he conducts is outstanding and very moving. He literally brings the orchestra and the music to life, in its fullest possibility. The world class musicians who have worked with him say that he brings out a potential in them that they did not know even existed. This is the beauty of what can occur when we individually choose to *presence* the life from within us rather just than re-present a version of it. Paying full attention to noticing what brings us alive and intentionally expressing that vitality draws out the same potential in others also. Karl Masur is a living example of this. By loving what he does, and choosing to wholly and fully express his love of life, his vitality becomes physically infectious for those who are in direct contact with him.

In an interview for a television documentary Masur said that: 'The world does not need more conductors, it needs more humans coming alive, more people singing with life, more people being human and conducting from that place of aliveness.' This very much resonates with Stephen Jenkinson's thoughts about where we are at in western civilisation right now. If we want to create livelier, more peaceful and loving societies we each need to find our own ways to come more alive and to be more fully human. The stepping-stones which have been laid out in this book give us some tools to 'conduct from a place of aliveness' and to fall in love with life. The more we can sense the life inside and outside of us, and become skilled at how to bring ourselves alive, the less dependent we are on our external circumstances to bring us alive.

In his book *Curious?* Todd Kashdan writes:

> Contrary to popular belief, our personality can change
> even if we are no longer in our awkward adolescent years.
> We can't change our genetic code, gender, age, ethnicity, or
> prior life events (the good, the bad, the ugly). But we can
> change how we think and which activities and goals we
> invest in.[9]

With gentleness, patience and persistence we can stop presenting 'perfect' versions of ourselves and let go of the need to be seen as anything other than we already are. Paying attention to experiencing ourselves and presencing our own life, exactly as it is, enables us to become more present, vulnerable and authentic. In turn, this practice creates new space for life to flourish and flow within us. And not only does it increase our possibility to feel alive, it exercises our ability to give life our full attention and to become more fully human.

7. The Ways in Which We Relate

When you are open and sincere, even the smallest thing can change your world, can shift your entire perspective ... your heart will become big enough to embrace the world as it is ... and somehow through that process, you become someone who has something revolutionary to offer this world – a truly open mind, an open heart, and an open consciousness.

Adyashanti, Falling Into Grace[1]

Suspending judgments

I am aware that I have a habit of judging people. Having spent some time reflecting on the ways in which I judge people I have noticed that my judgments tend to arise impulsively, without my choosing, and that they are related to my perception of people's values and emotional intelligence. For instance, I have noticed that very harsh assessments often spring into my mind quite spontaneously if I feel that a person with whom I am engaging is unnecessarily putting their own self-importance before the good of others. Similar judgments also seem to pop into my head when I am interacting with people who behave as though they value material goods more than the lives of those who helped make the items. These judgments also tend to surface when I am interacting with people who demonstrate a lack of 'soft skills', such as caring, the ability to listen attentively or to be genuinely empathic.

The way in which I judge the world acts like a double-edged sword: its cutting nature has helped me to establish a sense of right from wrong; the judgments have assisted me in directing my professional work away from being part of 'the problems' that I see in life and toward what I hope is the co-creation of a 'better' world; yet they often cause me personal pain. For example, when I judge a person's behaviour as arrogant, or have an encounter with a close friend who, despite their intimate involvement in my life, cannot empathise with me, not only do the judgments enter my mind unannounced in the form of thoughts, they bring with them an experience of actual physical discomfort inside my body. I have also noticed the action of judging can prevent me from getting to know life in terms of itself, as fixed judgments distance and separate me from the same world that I am trying to help. This happens especially when I apply judgment, not just to individuals, but to whole corporations, whole industries and, at times, even to whole nations.

As we saw in Chapter 1, the ways in which our minds habitually define life, such as organising our experience into a set of 'ideas', helps us to navigate our existence much more efficiently than if we had to embark on a journey of getting to know every part of life from scratch each and every time that we encounter it. Our judgments work in much the same way. Similarly to our 'organising ideas', there is often an essence of truth in them. By forming a judgment we are recognising familiar qualities in the way a person is acting that reflects *our understanding* of what it means-to-be that way, such as arrogant, angry or selfish. These judgments help us to distinguish between different forms of human behaviour, and to discern an appropriate way in which to respond. However, the way in which they fix our experience into a definitive shape makes the evaluation feel solid, absolute and impenetrable

As such, we often use judgments to jump to conclusions and to form opinions about the individuals, groups of people, or organisations that we are relating to. However, as with organising ideas, recognising something as familiar should be the point at which we *begin* our inquiries into the life we are experiencing, not end them. If we can learn to see our judgments as a starting point for getting to know life *as it is*, instead of seeing them as conclusions that distance us from the world, they can help direct us toward a closer understanding of the world in terms of itself.

For instance, instead of just judging a family member as 'selfish' and focusing our attention on that conclusion, we can put that judgment temporarily to one side and shift our attention toward observing the particular qualities of that person's behaviour and actions. This might include noticing the way the person concerned tends to eat the lion's share of a dessert or how they only seem to think of their own needs when planning family gatherings. We can use the particular instances of this behaviour that we perceive to be 'selfish' to reflect more deeply on the different circumstances and forms of expression in which we have noticed the 'selfishness' arising. On reflection we might notice a pattern arising in the times and way in which the behaviour emerges, such as noting that it only occurs when our whole family is gathered together. If we bring this pattern of behaviour to the person's attention we might find out that they actually consider themselves to be the least successful out of all of us. Consequently, this family member feels inadequate when the whole family is together. Therefore, in an effort to expand her sense of self-worth she ends up acting selfishly.

By noticing the ways in which this person acts 'selfishly', rather than solely focusing attention on our judgment of them being 'selfish', and stopping our inquiry there, we can lean back from the situation. This helps us to not take the behaviour personally and enables us to go further into the whole story that surrounds the behaviour we perceived. Suspending our judgments and paying full attention to how, when, and from where these judgments arise gives us the opportunity to notice the factors which contribute to them coming into being. These are the aspects of life, and of the living nature of the situation, that we would not have been able to notice if our inquiry had ended where it started, with our judgment. Through getting to know the behaviour as it is, and understanding the root issues that contributed to it coming into being, we open up the possibility to do something meaningful to resolve the issue.

Not only does this approach of exploring life beyond our judgments allow us to gain a deeper understanding of the person and the situation, it can also help us to interact with people that we might otherwise keep at a distance, such as those who have different political or economic interests from us, or those who have had a different kind of upbringing or education. Todd Kashdan affirms:

> Our default mode of thinking is mindlessness. We
> reflexively label and categorise things. For instance, other
> people get categorised as our friends and perhaps inner
> circle, or they are outsiders whom we tolerate, ignore or

shun. We form lasting impressions in mere seconds about
whether something is ugly or beautiful, or whether tasks
are boring or interesting.[2]

We can avoid these habits of labeling and judging people by holding
an awareness that there is more to seeing than meets the eye and
understanding that there is always another way of looking at, or
experiencing, something. This does not deny the existence of our
thoughts, opinions, instinctive feelings or hunches, or require us to
disregard our own beliefs, but it does allow us to potentially reduce
conflict by unlocking our ability to explore, and learn directly from,
the life that we are experiencing.

Judgments and labels are not the only tools that our minds use
in order to automatically make 'instant meaning' from our everyday
experiences. Assumptions, pre-conceptions, beliefs and prejudices
all contribute towards forming our instant impressions about the
world and can have a similar negative impact on our interpersonal
relationships. As we explored with the concept of organising ideas
in Chapter 1, noticing and then setting aside, or 'bracketing',[3] these
forms of instant meaning is essential if we wish to understand life
in terms of itself, whether it is individuals, groups of people, or even
widespread social, economic or environmental issues. Anyone who
wishes to work in the field of 'change' would benefit from this. Even
a simple sentence is loaded with assumptions and beliefs yet once we
become aware of these assertions we can open them up and explore
the situation deeper. In this way, bracketing allows the chance of
something newer to emerge. We can never completely 'bracket' life,
but we can try to always take responsibility for the ways in which our
own mind organises and defines the world.

Moving away from (bracketing) these forms of instant meaning-
making involves learning to describe our experience of life in terms
of itself, and this is very different to just telling people what we think
about life. Describing a part of life that we have been engaging with
can sometimes look and sound very similar to a judgment but there is a
crucial difference; judgments frequently spring to mind automatically
and, as they are only our mind's best guess at making meaning and
are influenced by our past experiences, these assertions are frequently
based on a superficial analysis of the situation. By contrast, when

we make a conscious effort to describe our experience by attentively noticing the way in which life is expressing itself, we allow life to speak for itself. For example, when we describe our experience of the way in which a certain person constantly draws attention away from others and towards themselves, and affirm our recognition that this person's behaviour appears to be narcissistic, we are noticing life as it is, not being overly critical or judgmental.

Whilst writing a chapter for the book *Stories of the Great Turning*, I vividly remembering one of my editors, Peter Reason, saying to me 'when you are writing, show, don't tell'. In other words, he was saying describe your lived experience in such a way that it leads people into the experience themselves, by letting life speak for itself. This is what careful description of our experience does, it allows life to speak for itself, to appear.

A living inquiry

So far, this book has attempted to demonstrate a way of seeing and relating to life that goes beyond theory. The people who have been referenced, such as Goethe, Henri Bortoft, and Iain McGilchrist, together with the authors of all the books that are mentioned, are not present simply because they appear to have 'good' ideas or draw similar conclusions about life. They are present because they all demonstrate a particular way of inquiring into life, into the lives of human beings and into the experience of being human. Rather than constructing a theory and striving to prove it, this book, and the researchers and authors cited, demonstrate a form of living inquiry that allows the part of life being studied to become its own theory and to show itself, on its own terms. In this way, the living nature of the inquiry allows that aspect of life to remain whole, and alive, and in so doing it enables us to learn from the dynamics and living context which bring that expression of life *into life* in the first place. This form of living inquiry allows life to appear and be understood, exactly *as it is*. As a result of studying life in this way, we can begin to notice the interconnections, relationships and patterns that express its essential nature.

A living inquiry is a dynamic way of seeing in action. Focusing our attention on life in this dynamic way can help us to deepen our understanding of every part of life that we encounter, including the people that we relate to on a daily basis. By using a form of living inquiry to focus on the ways in which people express themselves, beyond what we already think about them, we can begin to notice aspects of those people that we had not previously noticed, including qualities that are intrinsic to them as individuals. Inquiring into our relationships and interactions in this way can also help us to become aware of the more universal patterns in human nature that are inherent in the ways we each routinely behave and communicate. Instead of simply conducting our own personal living inquiries, we can also learn from researchers who have used this form of living inquiry on a much larger scale and, as such, have observed universal patterns and relationships that exist within, and shed light on, our own ways of behaving, relating and communicating.

For example, John Gottman, professor emeritus at the University of Washington, has spent his life exploring marital stability and relationships by leading, and reviewing, scientific studies that directly observe the behaviour of couples. As a result of this work Gottman noticed qualities and patterns of behaviour that are expressed repeatedly in unhappy marriages and relationships. What is especially important in relation to *First Steps to Seeing* is the form of inquiry that Gottman used and the way in which he approached the phenomenon of unhappy couples, which was to explore the interaction of couples as a whole. Instead of only researching failing, or unhappy, relationships, he included in his studies both couples whose marriages ended in divorce, and also couples who stayed together and were happy.

Gottman began his inquiries by using a *post hoc* analysis study of existing research to help him to identify specific behavioural patterns in couples. *Post hoc* analyses are used in order to discover patterns and/or relationships within a phenomenon. These patterns and relational qualities are likely to remain undetected if the research relies upon a more reductionist scientific method, such as first proposing a prediction or hypothesis and then attempting to prove it. Using a *post hoc* analysis to search for patterns within existing data allowed Gottman to gain a sense of which forms of behaviour might contribute toward the unhappiness in a relationship and thus lead toward the action of divorce. He then set out to explore these behavioral patterns in more depth by creating the conditions for them to be observed whilst appearing naturally, that is from within the interactions of couples as they went about their everyday lives.

This included carrying out studies in research facilities, which have been nicknamed the 'Love Lab' where couples were observed, living in an 'apartment lab' at the University of Washington.[4] The studio apartment appears to be just a regular living space, it looks out on to a lakeside park and contains all the usual fittings and furnishings that an average home would contain. In this way, the couples being studied are led to feel at home and to go about life as usual. To catch a glimpse of their natural behaviour, in action, the 'love lab' contains hidden cameras and the couples each wear a microphone and have a Holter monitor strapped to their chest. Using videotapes, questionnaires and live observation, each couple's daily life is monitored in action, whether they are talking, trying to solve problems, arguing or simply being together.

The studies that Gottman and his team carried out in the 'love lab' not only looked at the couple as a whole, they also researched aspects of the individuals as a whole, such as measuring heartbeats, stress hormones and monitoring the functioning of their immune systems. From this living inquiry Gottman noticed certain forms of behaviour that tend to appear in unhappy relationships and relationships that end in divorce. The most corrosive negative behavior patterns that he identified, which he calls 'The four horsemen of the apocalypse', are criticism, contempt, defensiveness and stonewalling.[5]

Rather than working to prove or even predict a hypothesis Gottman engaged in a process of becoming familiar with the phenomenon of an unhappy relationship as it expresses itself, in its natural environment, through the couples themselves. Through creating a living space for the couples that was as natural as possible, the behaviour could be studied in terms of itself, and on its own terms – allowing the behaviour itself to become its own theory. By then searching for patterns and relationships between the ways in which the different sets of couples behaved, Gottman noticed that the corrosive negative behaviour patterns that he and his team observed are significant aspects of human behaviour which *belong* together with unhappy relationships and divorce.

Instead of using a hypothesis to dissect and separate the data and then impose a connection by putting parts of it back *together,* Gottman studied the phenomenon as a whole and allowed the intrinsic connections to authentically appear on their own terms. The study shed a crucial light on aspects of being human, and the dynamics of human relationships, that are true to the essential nature of human beings – in much the same way that Goethe's inquiries revealed new insights into the intrinsic relationships that exist *between* light, darkness and colour.

The work of both Goethe and Gottman demonstrates the living dynamics of life that can appear when a living inquiry is used *to study* life. Both offer us the possibility of extending our own understanding of life by pointing us directly towards the intrinsic patterns and connections that they each noticed appearing whilst studying these phenomena.

Similarly, by studying hundreds of different conversations of every kind, another group of researchers, the authors of the book *Difficult Conversations,* have shed a new light on the ways in which human beings express themselves and relate to each other through conversation. One of the dynamics that they have noticed is that 'there is more to what we hear than meets our ears'. It is that piece of research that we will explore next.

More to hearing than meets the ear

Similar to the way in which there is 'more to seeing than meets the eye', the words that we 'hear' during a conversation with another person represent just the utmost tip of a very complex iceberg. By exploring what lies beneath that tip, and delving into the layers of our experience, we can challenge our habitual ways of responding to and relating with other people. The book *Difficult Conversations – How to Discuss What Matters Most* (by Stone, Patton and Heen) is a groundbreaking text that addresses ways of developing effective methods of communication. The text is required reading for many in senior management and epitomises the most comprehensive account that I have come across in terms of describing the underlying qualities, complexities, and patterns involved in human dialogue and communication.

The original inspiration for the book reflected the authors' desires to help negotiators in crisis situations, such as those involved in complex legal battles or international conflicts. By drawing on the wealth of their combined lived experience in business, law and international relations, together they conducted a living inquiry into the nature of conversations which has allowed patterns and insights to emerge that are intrinsic to the act of communicating itself, and inherent in all conversations. By shedding light on the layers and ingredients that make up conversations, which if left unnoticed can make dialogue difficult, they have given us the possibility of extending our understanding of the conversations we experience in everyday life.

In *Difficult Conversations* the authors initially suggest that every conversation has an intrinsic structure that is made up of three distinct aspects, which they call different 'conversations' – the 'what happened' conversation, the 'feelings' conversation and the 'identity' conversation. They describe, in great detail, the way in which the words we hear spoken by the other person are actually a mixture of how that person has responded to what they *thought* happened, the ways in which those events have challenged their identity (how they perceive themselves) and the feelings that were triggered by both of the above. The authors suggest that by having an awareness of these three distinct aspects, and actively exploring them for ourselves, we can avoid routinely sliding into conflict, and we can transform difficult conversations into learning experiences.

For instance, if a friend engages us in a difficult conversation by presenting us with a list of grievances as 'proof' that we do not appreciate or respect them, such as leaving the house late for an appointment, forgetting to mention that we added a personal item to the household shopping list and staying on the house phone for 'too long', it can leave us feeling hurt and angry. The friend in question has presented us with a list of our actions that they *have* actually experienced. We were late, we were on the phone for two hours, and we did add a personal item onto the household shopping list. However, in presenting these actions to us in such as way that suggests we were wrong, or intended them badly, the person has added a layer of meaning *on top* of our actions that they presume to be true, but this layer of meaning is not true in terms of the actions themselves.

Rather than our friend sharing the processing that they used to make meaning out of the situation, such as describing the feeling of hurt and the anxious emotions that arose within them when *thinking/*

presuming that our actions *meant* that we were not considering their feelings, our friend just presented us with the final conclusion of this meaning-making; that our actions were inconsiderate and disrespectful. The result of layering meaning on top of our actions without inquiring into *our* story of events prevents the person from understanding the true nature of the situation. If they had openly inquired into our experience they could have found out that we were late because of a sleepless night caused by the recent break-up with our partner; that the phone call was long because it was the first time we had spoken to our mother in over a month; and the personal item was on the shopping list because we had searched all over the city for it unsuccessfully, and having found the item online, had added it to the shopping list with the intention of letting the person concerned know straight away but had simply forgotten.

The events that our friend listed during the difficult conversation *had* happened but, in this case, the meaning that they interpreted from them was true only to their own inner processing of the events and not to the events themselves. Understanding that the structure of this one conversation is comprised of three distinct aspects can help us to explore what the other person *thought* happened, and the ways in which their feelings and identity were affected by those thoughts, rather than just taking their words at face value. This way of 'leaning back' during a conversation can help us to take the other person's attack less personally and potentially reduce any extreme habitual reactions that might otherwise cause us pain and suffering. Exploring the layers of the other person's experience, or story, also allows us to refrain from being overwhelmed, and yet still attempt to understand their story without abandoning our own.

Of course, when we are in the middle of a difficult conversation, remembering that there is 'more to hearing than meets the ear' is easier said than done. However, with practice, holding an awareness of these three different aspects, whilst we are in conversation with another person, can potentially improve the way in which we relate to them in the present moment and also possibly improve the quality of our overall relationship.

Another ingredient that affects the way in which we communicate, that *Difficult Conversations* addresses, is the exclusive nature of logic on which everyday perception relies. The linear quality of this logic leads to a belief that in any discussion, one person is right and therefore the other person *must* be wrong. It can be very difficult to remain curious about another person's story when we feel so strongly about our own, especially if we are under the illusion that only one of the stories can actually be right. As a way of moving beyond the limiting nature of this type of logic, especially when the other person's story feels so different to our own, the authors of *Difficult Conversations* recommend an exercise, which they call the 'And Stance'.[7]

When we are in conversation, feeling certain that our story is 'right' shuts out the possibility of understanding the other person's story. We usually think that if we accept another person's story it follows that we must abandon our own, but who is 'right' between someone who loves to walk in the full sunlight and someone who prefers to stay in the shade? Who is right between someone who loves to live in an extremely tidy house with minimalist decoration, and someone who likes to live in a house full of ornaments, paintings and ornate furnishings? The answer is a paradox, it is no-one *and* everyone, it is not an either/or, it is both/and (both of them and neither of them). This is what the 'And Stance' is. It embraces a different kind of logic; one that is inclusive and can accept two seemingly opposite points of view simultaneously. This does not mean that we need to pretend that the other person's point of view is 'right' but it does make it possible for us remain open and curious enough to explore the details of the other person's story, regardless of what we think *about* it.

When we let go of the need to accept or reject the other person's story we can work to understand it as it is. This can help us figure out what matters to both of us, to realise that how each of us feels is important and thus learn that both stories matter. In *Difficult Conversations* the authors affirm:

> The And Stance is based on the assumption that the world is complex, that you can feel hurt, angry and wronged, *and* they can feel just as hurt, angry, and wronged. They can be doing their best, *and* you can think that it's not good enough. You may have done something stupid, *and* they will have contributed in important ways to the problem as well.[8]

The value of this way of relating to other people is that it enables us to transcend our limited form of habitual logic and allows seemingly paradoxical thoughts and beliefs to sit side by side within our understanding, without us feeling as though we need to exclude or diminish any of them. This way of relating also makes it possible for us to assert the full strength of our thoughts and feelings without reducing the validity or strength of someone else's, and means that we do not need to give up anything just to hear how someone else's thoughts, ideas or beliefs differ from our own. The 'And Stance' is a powerful place to come from when we are in a difficult conversation as it enables us to be both compassionate and clear. For example, if we are putting an end to an intimate relationship our approach could include the following: Ending this relationship is painful for me *and* I'm sorry *and* I still want to break up *and* I know that this isn't how we expected this to end *and* I still need to do it ... and so on.

Restorative justice

In a similar way to the habitual labels, judgments and definitions that our minds produce, blame is often a conclusion that we reach when our minds routinely react to a situation in a simplistic manner. When we judge a situation and assign blame, we look to the past and uncover everything that we think we already know about it. However, if we wish to deepen our understanding of the situation and explore the dynamics and ingredients that contributed towards it coming into being, we need to move beyond our habit of reactively assigning blame. As with organising ideas, setting aside blame opens us up to noticing the complexities in a situation that we may not be able to *see* straight away.

Instead of blaming a person for causing us to feel a certain way, such as hurt or disappointed, we can open ourselves up to exploring the ways in which we may have contributed to the matter. Or if we are assigning blame on a wider scale, we can investigate how our communities or our society may have contributed in some way. For example, if we explore our habit of blaming corporations for ruining the planet, when we look closer we may realise that we contribute to this ourselves by buying their products and services. Or if we find ourselves blaming poverty on the government, as a result of exploring the ways in which poverty comes into being, we may realise that by buying houses to let, and charging the highest possible rent for them, we are contributing to the rising cost of living, which is a key aspect in the creation of poverty.

Understanding the ways in which we potentially contribute to a problem isn't just good practice, it is necessary if we wish to understand life as it is. This is useful, and crucially important, when our goal is to understand what is happening so that we can improve the situation, work together and do things differently. The authors of *Difficult Conversations* affirm that: 'Focusing on blame is a bad idea because *it inhibits our ability to learn what's really causing the problem and to do anything meaningful to correct it*'.[9] This is especially pertinent in regards to sustainability, social justice, and the environmental movement, which routinely focus on assigning blame when their actual aspirations are to accomplish understanding and to make a genuine difference in the world.

In some situations, such as the legal battles that occur in our courtrooms, the focus on blame is essential.

> Assigning blame publicly, against clearly articulated legal or moral standards, tells people what is expected of them and allows society to exercise justice ... but even in situations that require a clear assignment of blame, there is a cost.[10]

Once blame becomes a goal, understanding becomes the casualty. Blame stops us from inquiring any further or deeper into the nature of the situation and often leaves the accused less open and less willing to apologise. If we seek only to blame and not to learn, we exclude the possibility of figuring out how and what contributed to the situation. This can hinder the genuine resolution of issues and leave damaging behaviour, attitudes, systems and circumstances undiscovered.

On an interpersonal, and societal, level the practice of 'restorative justice' is an example of the way in which we can set blame aside in order to gain a deeper understanding of the situation and the impact that the offence has had on the individuals involved. This is a process whereby an offender meets their victim and engages in a dialogue. It is an attempt for both to move on with their lives more positively and productively, a kind of mutual rehabilitation. Restorative justice is used by the police in some areas of the United Kingdom as an alternative to criminal sentencing. I learned about this procedure as a result of watching a documentary which showed restorative justice in action, in which I was particularly struck by a meeting between a teenage 'offender' and a middle-aged woman.

The police had arrested the teenager after he and his group of friends had been caught harassing the woman outside her home. At the beginning of the meeting both the teenager and the woman were very guarded. They seemed to be relating not to each other, but to their own habitual labels of the other. The teenager saw the lady as a 'stuck up old woman', and the lady saw the teenager as an 'offensive young hooligan'. At the beginning of their encounter the teenager had his head down and was acting as if he was the victim. This all changed when the lady asked him how he would feel if this incident had happened to his mother. The teenager's reactions changed immediately in tone and expression, both physically and verbally. His whole appearance softened, he began to make eye contact and he started to open both his body language and also his mind. In response to this significant change in the teenager the woman started to change in a similar way. As they relaxed, both the woman and the teenager began to directly relate to their experience of each other as individuals, in that moment, rather than sticking intently to what they thought *about* the other. This allowed the 'victim' and the 'offender' to set blame to one side and to allow their experience in the present moment to inform and expand their understanding of each other. The encounter between these two people started in hostility and conflict, yet ended in some sense of common understanding and, very surprisingly, even finished with an embrace.

Another, more well-known, example of successful restorative justice occurred when a long standing house burglar from London was completely changed after meeting with the last man that he had robbed. In their meeting the victim described his experience of the robbery to the house burglar, detailing the nature of the constant fear that had surfaced for him since his home was broken into and expressed how this fear continued to deeply affect not only him but also his family. Both the London burglar and his victim were so moved during their meeting in 2002 that they remained friends and now they even work together. In 2008 these two men set up a charity together called *Why me?*[11] which promotes the use of restorative justice. Despite the awful events that had occurred in both their lives, when these individuals connected with their direct, living experience of the other, they were able to side-step blame, gain fresh insight into why the break-in happened and transform the ways in which they both understood, and related to, each other.

In the specific case of justice, and in our overall daily lives, every time that we definitively label a person as angry or arrogant, as poor or peculiar, as uneducated or underprivileged, we miss the possibility of understanding the ways in which they have come to be as they are. Although they are bringing to our awareness ways of being that we recognise, the judgments, labels and blame that we assign to the people around us are only ever our minds 'best guess' at making sense of *what* it is that we are experiencing. Any attempt at defining experience in this way acts like a full stop, or a dead end, and prevents us from learning anything further. When we notice and set aside these habitual reactions of our mind's and emotions, we can choose instead to engage in a living inquiry of life. By switching the focus of our attention to exploring the ways in which a part of life is expressing itself we allow the possibility of fully getting to know life, in terms of itself, to emerge.

The process of 'thinking about thinking', that conducting a living inquiry into our own habits of thought and perception requires, is known as 'meta-cognition'. By using meta-cognition to explore our thinking and its relationship to our feelings, behaviour and ways of communicating we can create the conditions for insights regarding everyday perception to emerge and we can shed light on collective perceptual 'blind spots'. In his highly informative book on the subject of attention, *Focus – The Hidden Drive of Excellence*, Daniel Goleman discusses shared blind spots in relation to social discrimination. He writes that:

> Inequity in a society fades into the background, something we habituate to rather than orient toward. It takes effort to shift it back into our collective focus.[12]

By noticing the parts of life that we are usually unconsciously unaware of, such as the details and complexities of being human that the authors of *Difficult Conversations* and the work of psychologist John Gottman have shown us, we can allow a more accurate, cohesive, dynamic understanding of life to emerge, individually and collectively. Together this empowers us to learn what is really at the root of the personal, interpersonal and societal problems that we face and greatly increases our ability to find meaningful resolutions to these problems.

8. A Dynamic Way of Seeing At Work

> Your work is a gift. This is a radical idea because it changes how you think about your work. It changes *why* you work, *what* you can make and even *who* you work for. When your work is a gift, your goal is no longer to satisfy a boss or a client – or even to gain a paycheck. *You now work to make yourself happy* – and in turn speak directly to your audience because you now give them something of *value*. A part of yourself.
>
> *Hiut Denim Company Yearbook[1]*

In this chapter I will introduce four examples of 'work' that I am very passionate about, these include: a research project in economic development; an educational initiative for mainstream schools; a scientific research institute; and a denim manufacturer. The key to these projects, and the link between them, is that each one gives full attention, to the way in which its activities are designed and carried out, and is not just solely concerned with what is done. In this way, these projects provide examples of a dynamic way of seeing *at work*.

Each of the four projects outlined in this chapter has been founded or co-founded by individuals who I loosely refer to as, 'Experts of Experience'. This term is designed to express the depth of lived experience that each individual has within their own field, and the way in which, by learning through experience, each of these people has developed a deep understanding – or living knowledge – of their particular discipline. A key point to note is that throughout their careers each one of these 'experts of experience' has become aware of the limiting habits of thought and practice which inform 'business as usual' within their field and have made a conscious effort to move beyond these restrictions. As a result, the projects that have emerged from their lived experience are an expression of meta-cognition, living inquiry and living knowledge in action.

To clarify my intention, by presenting these people alongside their projects I am not considering the individuals as more, or less, important than the projects themselves, or those who co-founded or carry out the projects with them. I am merely trying to illustrate the way in which systemic change can *begin* with an individual. I would also like to add that as much as I am passionate about these projects, and recognise their unique ways of working, I am aware that my experience of them is limited. Therefore, whilst I have attempted to be as accurate and informative as possible, these case studies serve only as a welcoming introduction, designed to spark direct inquiries into the actions of the projects themselves.

Each of these projects demonstrates an understanding of life from the *inside* out. By using living knowledge to put the needs of life itself at the very centre of professional practice, each project shows us ways in which life can, and does, thrive. In doing so these projects bravely challenge the status quo and reveal ways in which we too can begin to address some of the many global issues that we currently face; within our own, local environment and from our own doorsteps and workplaces. By bringing a tremendous degree of care and attention to the work that they do, at each and every level possible, each of these projects and people provides an example of a truly revolutionary way of working; the root of which is learning to see life in terms of itself.

Re-imagining economics: Manfred Max-Neef and Human Scale Development

In the twenty-first century, governments, mainstream media and businesses all over the world routinely express the idea that it is a combination of money and consumption that enables us to meet our individual needs as human beings. In turn this has perpetuated the common belief that earning more money and buying more 'stuff' is the most logical route to meeting our needs and being happy. In recent years this belief has consistently been proved false, as Colin Tudge points out: 'Above the level of abject poverty, more wealth has remarkably little impact on wellbeing. Yet our whole society is wedded to the ideal

143

of personal accumulation and wealth'.[2] Rather than satisfying our very real and complex set of individual human needs, the perpetual reinforcement of capitalist values, and profit dependent financial mechanisms, often lead us to consume products and services which not only *do not* meet our needs, they actually inhibit these needs being met.

The Chilean economist Manfred Max-Neef was a teacher of mine at Schumacher College. After some time spent working as an economist for Shell in the 1950s, Manfred left the industry in order to devote himself to studying the problems of 'developing' countries.[3] He did this by working on the ground with monetarily poor communities in Latin America, via United Nations organisations and various universities, such as the University of Berkeley in California. Having been inspired by 's *Small is Beautiful*, in the 1980s Manfred developed two ways of thinking about economics, and economic development, that not only present a deep, authentic understanding of people, in terms of themselves, but have enabled hundreds of small groups and communities around the world to pro-actively assess their genuine human needs themselves, and to explore how those needs can be best met in a local context.

The first of these new ways of thinking about economics was called 'barefoot economics', where Manfred proposed that a local economy can only be fully understood by immersing oneself in a lived experience of the particular environment which was under consideration. His second way of thinking was described as 'Human Scale Development', which offers an in-depth assessment of basic human needs while providing a participatory method for local communities to develop in order to reflect on their own needs, and identify the ways in which those needs can be satisfied, inhibited and violated. When asked in an interview in 2010 what 'barefoot economics' is, Manfred replied:

> ... a metaphor, but a metaphor that originated in a concrete
> experience ... I was standing in the slum. And across me,
> another guy was also standing in the mud – not in the
> slum, in the mud. And, well, we looked at each other, and
> this was a short guy, thin, hungry, jobless, five kids, a wife
> and a grandmother. And I was the fine economist from
> Berkeley, teaching in Berkeley, having taught in Berkeley
> and so on. And we were looking at each other, and then

> suddenly I realized that I had nothing coherent to say to
> that man in those circumstances, that my whole language
> as an economist, you know, was absolutely useless.[4]

Throughout his career, Manfred felt that the economists he encountered were convinced that they 'knew' everything about poverty, yet still did not *understand* it. In 1983, two years after the publication of his book *Outside Looking In: Experiences in Barefoot Economics*, Manfred won the Right Livelihood Award – which is also known as the 'alternative Nobel prize'. In order to take economics away from its conventional habitat of clean, orderly offices, in faraway places – full of people consumed by abstract theories, quantitative methodologies and financial statistics – Manfred spent the prize money from his award creating a research centre in Santiago de Chile which could put the feet of economists firmly back 'in the mud'. This was the Centro de Alternativas de Desarrollo (Centre for Alternative Development or CEPAUR).

Manfred spent many years with colleagues at CEPAUR exploring the concept, and experience, of poverty from the ground up. During this time Manfred and his team recognised and distinguished a detailed set of nine authentic human needs that they propose are *common to us all*, regardless of our nationality, education, and social, or financial, status. What is especially unique, and ground-breaking, in regards to this research is that the set of needs which Manfred and his colleagues distinguished go far beyond that of our immediate physical need for subsistence and cover the whole spectrum of our human experience, including emotional needs, social needs, intellectual needs and so on. In order to communicate these insights in a form that was easily accessible, yet still reflected the nature of their complexity, Manfred's team organised their findings into a matrix.

The 'needs/satisfiers' matrix (see Figure 4) has two axes; the horizontal axis lists the actions through which needs can be met, these include 'being', 'having', 'doing' and 'interacting'. Whereas the vertical axis lists the nine basic needs that were identified by Manfred and his team. These basic human needs are: Subsistence, Protection, Affection, Understanding, Participation, Creation, Idleness, Identity and Freedom. The boxes in the body of the matrix then contain suggestions of 'satisfiers' that can meet the basic human needs.

Needs / satisfiers matrix

	Being (qualities)	Having (things)	Doing (action)	Interacting (settings)
Subsistence	Physical, emotional and mental health	Food, shelter, work	Work, feed, procreate, clothe, rest/sleep	Living environment, social setting
Protection	Care, adaptability, autonomy	Social security, health systems, right, family, work	Cooperate, plan, prevent, help, cure, take care of	Living space, social environment, dwelling
Affection	Respect, tolerance, sense of humour, generosity, sensuality	Friendships, family, relationships with nature	Share, take care of, make love, express emotions	Privacy, intimate spaces of togetherness
Understanding	Critical capacity, receptivity, curiosity, intuition	Literature, teachers, educational and communication policies	Analyse, study, meditate, investigate	Schools, families, universities, communities
Participation	Adaptability, receptivity, dedication, sense of humour	Responsibilities, duties, work, rights, privileges	Cooperate, propose, dissent, express opinions	Associations, parties, churches, neighbourhoods
Idleness	Imagination, curiosity, tranquility, spontaneity	Games, parties, spectacles, clubs, peace of mind	Day-dream, play, remember, relax, have fun	Landscapes, intimate spaces, places to be alone, free time

Creation	Imagination, boldness, curiosity, inventiveness, autonomy, determination	Skills, work, abilities, method, technique	Invent, build, design, work, compose, interpret	Spaces for expression, workshops, audiences, cultural groups
Identity	Sense of belonging, self-esteem, consistency	Symbols, language, religion, values, work, customs, norms, habits, historical memory	Get to know oneself, grow, commit oneself, recognise oneself	Places one belongs to, every day setting, maturation stages
Freedom	Autonomy, passion, self-esteem, open-mindedness, tolerance	Equal rights	Dissent, choose, run risks, develop awareness, be different from, disobey	Temporal/ spatial plasticity (anywhere)

Figure 4. Human Needs Matrix. Reproduced with permission from Manfred Max-Neef, Economics Unmasked. From Power and Greed to Compassion and the Common Good (Totnes: Green Books, 2011).

Having two separate axes allowed the matrix to show the intrinsic connection *between* the ways in which we can meet our needs and the nine basic human needs which need to be met. This particular design helps to express the complex, living context of human needs and the dynamic, interconnected ways in which they are satisfied. The 'living context' of human needs (as laid out in the matrix) includes, *what* the basic human need is, such as, 'subsistence', *how* we can meet that need, such as looking after our physical health, what we need *to have* access to in order to meet it, such as food and shelter, what we need *to do* to meet the need, such as eating and resting, and *which* surroundings we need to be in, or interact with, to get the need met, such as a living environment with clean air and water.

Flexibility (or we could say, room for life to change and evolve) is intentionally built into the matrix as the 'satisfiers', which are contained in the middle boxes of the table, are not exhaustive and can be added to or altered according to the particular life circumstances of the individuals and communities who might use the matrix to assess their needs.

Through an immersion in community life Manfred and his team were able to distinguish a difference between our human needs and the ways in which those needs are satisfied. This led them to propose that the fundamental human needs which they identified are finite, few and classifiable, and can be recognised in all cultures and throughout all historical periods. The team suggested that what changes over time and across cultures, is the means by which the needs are satisfied, not the needs themselves. For instance, a person living in a rural English village in the seventeenth century would have satisfied the need for 'participation' at a local level, through, for example, families, the village community and maybe political or religious groups. Whereas a person living in the same geographical location in the twenty-first century would have the option of satisfying their need for participation on a much wider scale, such as being part of a school, college or university, engaging with groups of people via the internet, or physically travelling further afield, by car, bus, rail or even by air, to participate in shared-interest groups.

The holistic approach that Manfred and his team undertook in order to understand human needs, in terms of themselves, has revealed that although we each share the 'same' universal needs, that they can be satisfied in very different ways – many of which, such as affection, identity and participation, are not tied to money. By observing the authentic satisfaction of basic human needs, in their living context, another insight that emerged from this research is that our needs form a system, not a hierarchy:

> ... all human needs are interrelated and interactive. With the sole exception of the need of subsistence, that is, to remain alive, no hierarchies exist within a system.[5]

In order to further illustrate the systemic nature of human needs, Manfred and his team also distinguished a range of 'satisfiers' which illustrate the dynamic ways in which our needs are satisfied. These 'satisfiers' have varying characteristics and are classified as follows:

1. violators or destroyers
2. pseudo-satisfiers
3. inhibiting satisfiers
4. singular satisfiers
5. synergistic satisfiers

Violators violate, or destroy, our ability to get our needs met; pseudo satisfiers are false (or counterfeit) satisfiers that pretend to meet a need but do not; inhibiting satisfiers hinder our ability to satisfy a need; singular satisfiers satisfy only one need at a time and do not directly impact any of our other needs; and synergistic satisfiers satisfy more than one need at once.

Manfred considers synergistic satisfiers as the 'ultimate' form of satisfier and often uses the example of a mother breastfeeding her baby to illustrate the way in which they work. The act of breastfeeding is carried out because a newborn baby has a basic need for subsistence, and this is satisfied through the baby being breast fed milk. However, aside from the need for subsistence, the action of breastfeeding also satisfies other equally important needs *simultaneously* (or synergistically), such as the need for affection, protection and identity.

The human needs matrix and list of satisfiers can be used as a self-diagnostic exercise for individuals and local community groups who would like to explore what they genuinely need, and to investigate how they can authentically satisfy those needs within their own local area. Similarly, the matrix can also be used as a tool, in diagnosis, planning, assessment, and evaluation, to study those who will be directly impacted by development projects. Shortly after being published, first in Spanish and two years later in English, the studies on Human Scale Development generated immediate interest and enthusiasm. 'Ever since the results of the project were published in a Spanish edition of Development Dialogue in 1986, under the title of "Desarrollo Escala Humana: una opción para el futuro", it has attracted wide attention in Latin America'.[6] The documents outlining Human Scale Development and The Theory of Fundamental Human Needs were picked up by communities, including peasant and Indian communities in South America, and shared on the ground with remarkable speed. Manfred prides himself on the fact that the materials are some of the most widely photocopied resources in Latin America:

> We used to arrive in Andean communities to be
> approached by local leaders with a photocopy of a
> photocopy of a photocopy, almost unreadable, ready
> to discuss whether their interpretation was correct and
> whether their projects satisfied the philosophy of Human
> Scale Development. It was moving to witness how such
> marginal communities adopted the principles and designed
> local development projects that conventional experts
> would have been unable to conceive of. Many of those
> projects have survived and flourished.[7]

Not only does Human Scale Development provide individuals, communities and organisations with a comprehensive framework from which to comprehensively explore authentic human needs but it can also help us to radically alter the way in which we understand 'poverty'. As a result of immersing himself in 'poor' communities, by experiencing them directly – staying, living, eating and being in them – Manfred was able to gain a deeper understanding of the phenomenon that we commonly define as 'poverty'. Through recognising the systemic (non-hierarchical) relationship between needs and the ways in which they are satisfied, the team identified that it is not just an inability to meet our need for subsistence that leads to poverty, but that if any need is left unmet, 'poverty' is created. Instead of looking at and talking about poverty from the outside, Manfred lived *with* it, and therefore gained an understanding of poverty from the inside:

> The traditional concept of poverty is limited and restricted,
> since it refers exclusively to the predicaments of people
> who may be classified below a certain income threshold.
> This concept is strictly economistic. It is suggested here
> that we should speak not of poverty, but of poverties. In
> fact, any fundamental human need that is not adequately
> satisfied, reveals a human poverty. But poverties are not

only poverties. Much more than that, *each poverty generates pathologies.*[8]

Through the 'eyes' of Human Scale Development, most of the social 'problems' we identify today, such as depression, alcoholism, eating disorders, unemployment, racial conflicts, and disaffected youths, can be seen as *pathologies.* This means that, if we look carefully, each 'problem' can be traced back to an array of fundamental human needs which are not being met. Paying attention to the unmet needs of individuals and groups of people makes it possible for us to resolve the problems that we perceive in the world around us at the root of the matter, rather than just medicating these people with partial 'solutions' that never really address the heart of the issue.

The living knowledge that Manfred and his colleagues gained, by exploring economics with their feet firmly 'in the mud', makes it possible for us to go 'upstream' and to meet poverties at their source; fundamental human needs that have been left unmet. We can then find ways in which to satisfy these unmet needs synergistically – ways that are suitable to, and sensitive to, the local social and environmental context.

In this way, Human Scale Development not only offers an alternative perspective on poverty, development and economics, it extends our understanding of *being human*, and what it means to understand life. In the book *Economics Unmasked*, which Manfred co-authored with the American physicist Philip B. Smith in 2011, he uses the experience of love to highlight the crucial difference between knowledge and understanding:

> We can, for instance, guided by our beloved scientific method, study everything there is, from theological, anthropological, sociological, psychological and even bio-chemical perspectives, about a human phenomenon called love ... But once we achieve that complete knowledge, we will sooner or later discover that we will never *understand* love unless we fall in love ... We will then be aware that we can attempt to understand only that of which we become a part.[9]

What is also especially pertinent with regard to the global crises we face today is the distinction that Manfred draws between growth and

151

development. 'Growth is a quantitative accumulation. Development is the liberation of creative possibilities'.[10] Manfred uses human beings as an example. At some point, our physical form stops growing, but as individuals, we can keep developing our skills, ideas and knowledge for as long, and as intensively, as we wish. Therefore, where human beings are concerned, growth has limits, but development does not. The same can be said for our economy. Development should not be defined by, and limited to, growth, economic or otherwise.

Manfred is also the author of a well-known hypothesis, called the 'threshold hypothesis'. This states that in every society there is a period in which economic growth brings about an improvement of the quality of life but only up to a point. This point is its 'threshold', beyond which, if there is more growth, quality of life begins to decline. This seems to be the situation that the majority of countries in the West are currently facing. However, I believe that the 'upstream' approach to meeting needs, and understanding poverty, economics and development, that Manfred and his team first developed in the 1980s still offers us more than a glimmer of hope for resolving the current social and economic issues of our time – from the ground up and from the inside out.

Reviving education: 'Learning in Depth' and the work of Kieran Egan

As we explored in the previous section of this chapter through the work of Manfred Max-Neef, there is a crucial difference between knowledge and understanding. To truly understand a part of life, we need to learn *with* it, not just learn *about* it. This involves becoming deeply and intimately acquainted with that particular aspect of life. As such, understanding cannot be formally taught, rather individuals need guidance in order to construct their own understanding. In schools today children are generally taught a body of knowledge that represents what we think we already know *about* the world. We tend to do this by teaching from textbooks and giving children information rather than exposing students to the parts of life that they are learning about. This teaches children to equate knowledge, and learning, with the memorisation of 'facts' while ignoring the child's capability to learn from the world in a self-directed way, through discovery and from their own experience.

Even though we are now in the twenty-first century, a fast-paced age of technology and information, many mainstream schools, colleges and universities act as though they are industrial factories, designed to manufacture learning. This 'factory' style of education emphasises conformity, rote-learning, and the testing of memorised 'facts'. It also espouses industrial values of uniformity, consistency, efficiency and mechanistic assembly, which it uses to force-feed our children, teenagers and young adults with information, as though they were battery hens destined for a supermarket shelf.

Instead of allowing true understanding to grow, the current industrial style of education uses forms of knowledge and methods of teaching that are both superficial and fragmented. The crisis of education is the subject of *The Educated Mind – How Cognitive Tools Shape Our Understanding*. In the introduction, the author Kieran Egan writes: 'The costs of our educational crisis, in terms of social alienation, psychological rootlessness, and ignorance of the world and the possibilities of human experience within it, are incalculable and heartbreaking'.[11]

I recently came across the work of Kieran Egan, who is a contemporary education philosopher and professor of education, whilst carrying out an inquiry into the work and ideas of Henri Bortoft. Having traced Henri's path back to a period in the 1960s spent working with the Institute for Comparative Studies (ICS, a research centre founded by the British mathematician and scientist J.G. Bennett), I realised that Henri's time there involved living and working with a small group of other scientists and researchers. Kieran Egan was a member of this group and he worked at ICS for a year together with Henri and the other researchers investigating educational methods.

Curious as to the paths that members of the group had taken, other than Henri, I spent some time exploring the careers and projects that had later unfolded. It was during this inquiry that I found myself particularly taken with the work and ideas of Kieran Egan. After studying in London and working as a research fellow at ICS, Kieran moved to the US to study education at Stanford and Cornell, and is now based at the Simon Fraser University in Canada. Through his years of immersion in the subject of education, Kieran has spent a great deal of time experiencing, studying, researching, teaching and writing about educational philosophies, theories, and practices. He also expanded his inquiries into the nature of understanding, drawing on wide ranging fields of thoughts, such as cultural and evolutionary history, anthropology and cognitive psychology. It seems that through immersing himself in the *life* of learning Kieran has uncovered some important principles, philosophies and common assumptions that are at the root of the issues we face in education today.

In his explorations of modern school education Kieran has come to recognise that mainstream schools are built around three main ideas, each of which is fundamentally incompatible with the other two:

> In the case of the modern school, three distinctive aims
> have attended its development. It is expected to serve
> as a significant agency in socializing the young, to teach
> particular forms of knowledge that will bring about a
> realistic and rational view of the world, and to help realize
> the unique potential of each child. These goals are generally
> taken to be consistent with one another, somewhat
> overlapping and mutually supportive ... however, each of
> these aims is incompatible in profound ways with the other
> two ... the more we work to achieve one of the school's
> aims, the more difficult it becomes to achieve the others.[12]

Having explored these three, often taken for granted, basic ideas upon which modern school education is based, and noticed the ways in which they interact with and contradict each other, Kieran deepened his inquiry into exploring the nature of understanding itself. From this inquiry a distinct pattern of learning and understanding emerged that appears to be intrinsic to human development. Kieran identified this pattern as a number of different 'intellectual stages' that occur throughout the course of a person's intellectual development, which he refers to as 'distinctive kinds of understanding'.[13] These 'understandings' that he identified, in the order of their natural development in the individual, are: somatic, mythic, romantic, philosophic, and ironic. Kieran suggests that each stage of 'understanding' develops its own set of 'cognitive tools' and that a genuine resolution to the problems that modern school education currently faces would be to allow the process of learning to reflect these natural stages of human development.

During his inquiries into learning and education Kieran also shed light on other limiting principles that constitute the ground upon which most school education is built. These include the idea that we should teach children by *starting* from what they already know and that we should lead from the simple into the complex. In *Getting It Wrong From The Beginning*, published in 2002, Kieran affirmed:

> How can one hold as a general development principle that human learning progresses from the simple to the complex when we see nearly all children mastering language and complex social rules while most adults can't program a VCR?[14]

In this book Kieran goes on to say that the principle of teaching children by starting from what they already know is one of the most persistent and powerfully influential principles that exists in education today. He writes:

> Nearly every teacher and professor of education I have encountered believes this principle. Most people assume it to be so obviously true that even to question it suggests a degree of nuttiness.[15]

The willingness of Kieran to pay attention to, and deeply question, the foundations of educational thought and practice has laid a series of much needed stepping stones for those of us who are interested in genuinely resolving the current mess that our educational system is in. However, the aspect of his work that I am most passionate about, and which sparked my interest the most, is an educational initiative, called 'Learning in Depth'. This initiative recently emerged from the Imaginative Education Research Group (IERG), which Kieran founded in 2001 as part of the Faculty of Education at the Simon Fraser University in Canada.[16]

After many years spent researching, '... how to engage students' emotions and imagination in the content of the curriculum'[17] Kieran and his team at IERG used their living knowledge of learning, and an in-depth understanding of the ways in which learning comes alive within children, to develop this innovative project-based educational initiative. As a result, 'Learning in Depth' (LiD) was designed to ensure that all students were guided to become 'experts' in *one* topic by the time they finish school and focuses on the depth, rather than breadth, of learning. Each child participating in the initiative is given a particular topic to study throughout their whole school life, such as apples, stars or religions and is encouraged to devote time to the topic each week.

The children are encouraged to experience this topic in as many ways as possible. For instance, if the topic was 'apples' the child would be free to eat an apple, to draw it, to see where and how it grows. The child could find out where the first ever apple tree was found, ask parents and friends what they think about apples and investigate how they use them, where they buy them, and so on. Whilst engaging in this discovery-led learning, the students document their findings week by week and gradually build a personal portfolio on the topic that they have been given. In this way, the LiD initiative leads children into the process of understanding life itself, as it is, by allowing them to engage with and freely explore their one topic throughout their whole school life.

Over the duration of their school life, as the child's skill set develops and expands, the ways in which they explore their topic can develop accordingly. For example, the topic of apples could be expanded to include a study of apple trees and their natural habitat, in which they could explore the best type of soil for cultivating apple trees, investigate the climates in which apple trees grow and map the countries in which apple trees are currently found. The student could also study the type of agricultural practices that are currently used to grow the apples and compare them to those that have been used in the past. Alternatively, if microbiology was of interest to the student, they could progress to researching the cellular structure of an apple, or if they were interested in health and fitness they could explore data concerning an apple's nutritional content and research recipes that included apples. On the other hand, if the student's interests turned towards art or culture they could explore famous paintings that included apples, or the cultural symbolism of apples in different countries and at different times in human history.

Gradually over sixteen or so years of studying the subject of 'apples', the student is given a golden opportunity to let their own personal interests drive and motivate their inquiry, and to develop an understanding of apples that reaches far deeper than any other topic that the child will cover during their entire time at school.

Focusing on just *one* topic does not mean that the student will only know about 'apples' or 'stars' or 'religions' at the end of their study. Each student will have established the essential skills involved in getting to know a part of life in depth and will have learned about other subjects and aspects of life in the process. For instance, not only will the child encounter knowledge from specific subjects such as art, history, anthropology, chemistry and mathematics, they will also have gained an understanding of the ways in which all these subjects interconnect. Studying apples for sixteen years does also not mean that the student is destined to have a career linked to this topic. However, the child will be able to apply their understanding of learning in depth to all other inquiries that they will carry out in later life.

LiD is primarily designed to capture the child's imagination and to develop a love for learning, this occurs by allowing the child to be motivated by their own curiosity and by giving them the opportunity to inquire at their own pace. The conventional approach to education tries to squeeze learning into a form that is the easiest and most convenient for us, as adults, such as sitting a child down for specific periods of time and just expecting them to absorb vast quantities of information and, therefore, 'learn'. However, in the Learning in Depth initiative, the life of learning is allowed to emerge, to be experienced, and thus, understood, in terms of itself, and on its own terms.

What is especially wonderful about LiD is that it is aimed at mainstream schools and designed to sit alongside the current curriculum. This gives teachers the opportunity to effect a change in educational methods, from the bottom up, without relying on top-down changes from governmental policies or curriculum design. LiD is also low-cost and low-maintenance. In this respect, the fact that LiD is not designed to be assessed is of crucial importance. The teacher's role is more one of being a 'port of call' for questions and guidance, which means that no extra administrative work is created.

The effectiveness of this initiative is already starting to show as LiD is fast becoming popular all over the world. Many schools begin by testing LiD in just one class but, when they experience how well the project is received by the students, the initiative often gets introduced into a number of other classes the following year. LiD started in 2008 with only two schools participating, and the number of children it reached grew to two thousand children by 2009.[18] The reach of the initiative has now become global and LiD continues to be implemented in mainstream schools all over the world today, including some schools based in the UK.

To date, researchers at IERG have reported that children usually take to the program with great enthusiasm, and they have been told by parents and teachers that within a few months LiD begins to transform the children's experience as learners.[19] One parent reported experiencing a remarkable growth in her son's learning shortly after participating in LiD at his school:

> As they studied their topics I began to realize that
> my son was commanding my attention with a new
> excitement in his voice. I couldn't help but be amazed
> by the conversations ... I was astounded by what he
> knew and how he was able to articulate this knowledge
> with such confidence ... He is in grade four this year
> and I know that Learning in Depth has aided in his
> extreme ability to comprehend new knowledge. I believe
> that because he was allowed to explore information
> about a topic . . . he became aware of his own ability to
> understand.[20]

Many other parents and teachers have also described the way in which the Learning in Depth initiative engages their children in a process of 'learning to love learning'.[21] Some parents observed that, since their children had become involved with LiD, they have had new and deeper levels of conversations with them, which they had never experienced prior to the children's participation in the initiative.

The broader aspirations for LiD include opening children up to the mystery of the world and the wonders that it contains. Kieran Egan also hopes that it may help children to develop the ability to discern fact from opinion. In his wonderful book on the subject, *Learning in*

Depth – A Simple Innovation That Can Transform Schooling, Kieran writes:

> I think people who have only the sketchiest sense of knowledge, because they know nothing in depth, easily confuse their wishes, needs, and opinions with knowledge, and in so doing create many of our most serious social and political problems.[22]

Our current mainstream education system generally tends to form individuals in such a way that they learn to stand at a distance from all that they think they know. It also inhibits the development of their inherent capacities to inquire into, to observe, participate with and to understand the world for themselves. When these capacities are left unused individuals are then naturally coerced into relying on 'authorities' to obtain knowledge, whether it is Google and Wikipedia, politicians, or the growing myriad of other individuals and organisations that have a vested interest in telling people what these 'authorities' think they need to know.

To gain a deep, genuine understanding of something we must allow that part of life to enter into us, and to come alive within us. This includes developing an understanding of the life of learning, and what it means to learn. I believe that the 'Learning in Depth' initiative does exactly this, in a low-cost, enjoyable way that is inherently teacher, parent and child-friendly.

Re-visioning science: The Nature Institute and the work of Craig Holdrege

I was taught by Craig Holdrege on the MSc in Holistic Science at Schumacher College in 2008. After joining our class for a week-long session with Henri Bortoft, Craig then spent the second week of term leading us into a 'living' way of inquiring into life, which enabled us to experience Henri's philosophical concepts in action. The 'container', and context, in which this form of living inquiry was introduced to us was Goethean Science, which is a science of qualities. To use Henri's phrase, Goethe's way of science aims at 'a conscious participation in nature.' Rather than investigating life as though it were a series of objects, Goethean Science is used to study parts of life, whether animals, plants or rocks, as expressions of living form. As it uses a phenomenological-type method of inquiry, this way of doing science strives to get to know living organisms in terms of themselves and endeavours to allow the part of life being studied to become its *own* theory.

Craig Holdrege is a biologist, educator and author, and conducts his living inquiries into life with a cautious and critical awareness of the ways in which '... intentions and habits of mind affect human understanding'.[23] Craig is also director and co-founder of the Nature Institute, a small, independent not-for-profit organisation in upstate New York. This institute acts as a forum for local, national, and international research and education, and it is here that he carries out his 'living' scientific inquiries into life. The scientific inquiries that Craig and his colleagues carry out involve studying organisms as living 'wholes'. Part of this process includes consciously striving to develop a living way of thinking that is as dynamic as the life that they study, both as individuals and as a whole institute.

The scientific research that Craig does takes two directions. In the first, he explores organisms, such as plants and animals, as whole, dynamic beings, and studies them 'in context' by investigating the way in which they are integrated within the larger web of life. Craig has written many papers on these studies of organisms, each of which demonstrates the ways in which the animal's, or plant's, unique features are interconnected and integrated within the context of that individual being as a whole. These studies really bring the nature of the organism to life on the page and are quite unlike any other 'scientific' papers that I have read. I remember being particularly taken by Craig's living inquiry into the life of the sloth, the '... most prevalent tree-dwelling mammal in Central and South America's rain forests'.[24] Having comprehensively studied the sloth as a whole, living form, which included attending to the environment in which it lives (its living context), Craig revealed the way in which the quality of 'slowness' is expressed through every part of the sloth's being.

In his wonderful essay, 'What does it mean to be a sloth?' Craig describes in detail the way in which all aspects of the sloth's biology and behaviour express this quality of slowness, whether it is the way it moves, its gestation period, the time it takes to digest food, or its slow growing teeth, to name but a few:

> The sloth develops slowly in the womb and has a long, slow
> life. It moves slowly through the crowns, feeding on the
> leaves that surround it from all sides, bathing, as it were,
> in its food source. The leaves pass through the animal at
> an almost imperceptibly slow rate. The sloth's stomach is
> always filled with partially digested leaves. Even its dung
> disappears slowly, despite the warm and humid rain forest
> climate that normally accelerates decomposition processes
> ... The sloth brings slowness into the world.[25]

Craig and the other researchers at the Nature Institute intentionally use a science of 'qualities' to study life because they recognise the way in which mainstream modern science has progressively moved further and further away from observing and studying parts of nature as whole living beings. Through the lived experience that they have gained from working in science and science education, these researchers have witnessed the way that science has gradually driven itself deeper into the laboratory in order to search for an underlying mechanistic basis of life.

Whilst teaching at Schumacher College, Craig described the way in which mainstream biology is full of mechanical explanatory metaphors and is always looking for the underlying 'mechanism' in living form. This way of doing science relies on causal thinking, which reduces life to linear mechanisms of cause and effect, even when investigating the life of living organisms. Craig believes that at the root of this mechanistic approach to science is the most prevalent collective habit of thought in the world today – a form of 'object thinking' that sees the world as if it consists only of objects. This way of thinking, which he believes remains invisible and unstated to the majority, strives to 'explain' life as though it were a series of separate objects, and as if each object represented 'things' made up of other 'things'. Having recognised the limitation that this way of thinking, and way of carrying out scientific studies, delivers, rather than attempting to explain the natural life that they study, the Nature Institute endeavours to bring the *qualities* of life to expression.

This act of bringing life to expression, rather than explaining it, is also demonstrated in the second strand of Craig's research at the Nature Institute, which focuses on the '... comprehensive and holistic understanding of organisms.' As part of this research Craig focuses on genetics and genetic engineering, but in a much broader, living context than is currently adopted by mainstream approaches to the subject. Rather than looking at 'genes' mechanistically, as though they were 'objects', he explores them in relation to the broader internal and external ecology (or context) of which they are a part.

As a result of exploring the subject of genetics 'in context', Craig and his colleagues at the Nature Institute, including Steve Talbott, have provided us with a new understanding of genetic 'inheritance'. In Craig's teachings he described the way in which genetic inheritance expresses itself through the organism as '... predisposed potential and ability to "other" in response to external conditions – it is not pre-determined – No-thing is inherited'.[26] By bringing to expression the ways in which chromosomes and DNA are constantly being reformed in relation to their inner and outer ecology, the work that Craig and his colleagues have done demonstrates the highly contextualised nature of a gene. Unlike a mechanistic view of the gene, which is static and fixed in an object-like way, the work of the Nature Institute demonstrates the gene's dynamic way of being, where continuity is present but not in a predetermined way.

In his teaching, Craig described how the way of 'object thinking' is expressed through the practice of genetic modification, which treats genes as though they are 'things' that are separate from the internal and external ecology that surrounds them. The mainstream understanding (in popular thought that is, not scientific inquiry) is that genetic engineering is a highly controlled and precise process but if we were to delve deeply into reports of scientific experimentation we would find that it most certainly is neither greatly controlled nor precise.

I was surprised to learn that genetic modification (GM) does not work in most areas. For the majority of the time GM turns organisms into very bizarre, disfigured versions of themselves. Very occasionally the changes are 'desirable,' which means that on the surface the modifications do not 'appear' to have caused any extreme changes. In other words, the external, physical form looks the same, yet the organism has been fundamentally altered in some way. For example, even though the plants of a GM crop appear to be the 'same' in terms of their physical appearance, the way in which the crop responds to its living environment may have been significantly changed, such as becoming resistant to extreme changes in temperature or resistant to pests.

The 'desirable' genetic modifications, which are few and far between, are integrated into organisms that will be cultivated for mass-production, such as corn, soya beans, cotton, or tomatoes, and then these GM organisms are introduced back into the natural environment. However, this is done without in-depth studies being carried out into the ways in which the genetic modifications unintentionally impact the organism or its environment.

As Craig argues, when we understand that an organism is a whole, we also understand that if we change the part, that we also change the *whole* – this goes for individual organisms and whole eco-systems. A lack of this understanding (of the wholeness of nature) is what Craig believes leads geneticists to mix genes that nature itself would never mix. What is most worrying to him is not the practice of GM itself but the disconnected mind of the human that it reflects. As he writes in *A Question of Genes: Understanding Life in Context*:

> Through such genetic manipulations we disturb the integrity of the organism as a whole. This follows from our willingness to consider organisms as conglomerations of separate traits. Transgenic organisms put our thinking on display. Object-thinking finds an especially stark reflection in the disjointed, erector-set character of such plants and animals.[27]

The book *Beyond Biotechnology – The Barren Promise of Genetic Engineering* which Craig co-authored with Steve Talbott, a senior researcher at the Institute, provides an accessible introduction to the complicated issues surrounding genetic engineering and its potential applications. In the book they challenge the common assumption that genetic engineering is a universal remedy that can help 'solve' global food and health problems. The authors also show the unintended effects that genetic modification has on both organisms and the environment as a whole:

> Putting the matter plainly: when foreign genes are introduced into an organism, creating a transgenic

organism (commonly called a genetically modified
or genetically engineered organism), the results for
the organism and its environment are almost always
unpredictable. The intended result may or may not be
achieved in any given case, but the one almost sure thing is
that unintended results – nontarget effects – will also be
achieved.[28]

Prior to co-founding the Nature Institute, Craig worked as a biology
teacher for over twenty years, and as a teacher trainer and mentor for
Steiner education for many subsequent years. What I find especially
inspiring about Craig's work is the way in which he is demonstrating a
form of living inquiry that is adequate to study the complex, dynamic
nature of living form. Not only are he and his colleagues at the Nature
Institute bringing our understanding of living organisms to *life* but
by being explicit about the way in which they are doing this, they are
carrying out a living inquiry into living inquiry itself. To those who
pay close attention, the way in which the institute describes, not just
its findings, but its approach to studying life can provide a pathway to
living knowledge for us to follow. This pathway cannot only be applied
as a new research method but also as a new educational methodology.
Aside from practising this particular way of studying life, Craig also
teaches this form of phenomenological inquiry as a way for us to get
out 'into the world and out of our minds, without losing our heads'.

In September 2012 I attended a weeklong course in the United
States with Craig and his wife Henrike Holdrege, entitled 'A Pathway
to Living Knowledge'. In the mornings we mostly worked with Craig
on phenomenological plant studies, and in the afternoons with
Henrike we studied various forms of projective geometry, discovering
the patterns of lawfulness that emerge from pure mathematics. From
the very beginning Craig encouraged us to reverse our habitual
approach to studying the world. He asked us to 'do something' and
then consider it, rather than to consider something in abstraction
and then do it. Craig described this phenomenological process as a
shift of focus, a turning toward something in the world where one
enters the methodology as a result of participating directly with the
phenomenon, and during that week in New York state, this is exactly
what we did.

Over a series of teaching sessions, both indoors and outdoors, we were encouraged to describe, as exactly as possible, the wildflower Golden Rod, which inhabited the surrounding sunlit meadows. After practising observing and describing the Golden Rod, in terms of itself, we were then asked to re-picture our experiences in our mind and to reflect on our observations. Then to gain an even broader, living picture of this organism we visited the different kinds of places in which the plants grew locally, such as crowded hedgerows and shady woodland. In this way we were able to observe the ways in which the plants manifested themselves 'the same but differently', according to the particular location and conditions that we observed them living in. It was astonishing to notice the huge contrast between the ways in which the plants grew in different locations. In the sunny paddock, the Golden Rod plants were bursting full of tiny yellow flowers, as though a firework had been set off and then freeze-framed. Whereas in the shaded woodland, which was only dappled with light, there was a much greater degree of spacing between the flowers, the plants were also smaller, with fewer branches, and the organs of the flowers even had a slightly different configuration.

Through this course in the US, and my time spent studying with Craig in the UK, I have had a lived experience of the wonderful way in which he leads people straight into an experience of life and then encourages them to reflect on their experience. This way of learning through discovery allows the world to speak for itself, and makes it possible for the life of the world to 'speak' directly to the students themselves. By attending to living organisms in this way a pathway to living knowledge and a living science for life emerges, from which we can begin to understand the wholeness of life. Craig also advocates this 'pathway' as a style of education for children. In *Thinking Like a Plant* he writes:

> This kind of learning takes time. You cannot rush from
> one animal to the next. You need to let it become for
> the children a presence, one illuminated through other
> presences. Having dwelled with a few animals is much
> more than having raced through an overview of the whole
> animal kingdom ... Educator Martin Wagenschein puts it
> this way: 'We recommend the *courage to leave gaps*, which

means the courage to be thorough and to dwell intensively on selected topics. So instead of evenly and superficially walking through the catalog of knowledge, step-by-step, we exert the right – or fulfill the duty – to really settle in somewhere, to dig in, to grow roots and take root ... The particular aspect we delve into is not a stage in a process, but a mirror of the whole.'[29]

I strongly believe that the Nature Institute's research, and way of thinking, is crucial in developing our own understanding of the way in which it is possible to get to know life *as it is*, on its own terms, as individuals, researchers and educators. Ultimately, I believe that this form of living inquiry, and living knowledge, is the only way in which mankind can become genuinely sustainable; as only through cultivating a type of thinking that is as alive as life itself, can we allow life to show us the ways in which it can, and does, thrive.

Re-designing business: Hiut Denim and the work of David Hieatt

When I was given my second job designing and developing underwear in Hong Kong in 2004, the vacancy came about as a result of the closure of a whole factory in Bristol. The company that hired me, The Stirling Group, was one of the leading clothing and underwear suppliers in the UK at the time, and owned a number of British factories, as well as design offices and warehouses. I was hired to 'replace' a whole department from the Bristol factory, which had been made up of machinists, pattern cutters, graders, designers and a product developer.

In order to complete a 'handover' between myself and the team in Bristol, I flew from Hong Kong to meet the product developer whose job I would be taking on, her name was Rose. Needless to say, the meeting was awkward. Not least because I was only twenty-three at the time and, partly due to the luck of already being based in Hong Kong, had just jumped ten years ahead on my career path, overnight. The discomfort wasn't helped by the fact that we both knew that the same beautiful line of luxury underwear that she had carefully developed over the years with her experienced team of local seamstresses and pattern cutters, would carry on without them. We also both knew that I would get these garments produced with far less heritage and collective experience, but for a lot less money.

The closure of the Bristol factory was part of The Stirling Group's attempt to fight the battle of becoming the 'cheapest' of its competitors. Eventually, it lost and finally went out of business in 2008. Ten years after visiting the factory in Bristol, and having left the lingerie industry far behind me, I came across a very similar story in the market town of Cardigan, in Wales. The town used to contain the biggest jeans manufacturer in the UK. For over three decades, four to five hundred people (a tenth of the town's four thousand inhabitants) used to produce 35,000 pairs of jeans per week, in just one factory. Then, one day in 2001, the clothing factory shut its doors, production was moved to Morocco and suddenly four hundred people in Cardigan became unemployed overnight.

This jeans factory had fought the same battle as the underwear factory that I had visited in Bristol, to become the 'cheapest', and it too had lost. The employees remained in the town, along with their skills and decades of combined knowledge and experience, but with no way of working these people, and the heritage of their trade, it became obsolete over night. That was until, about a decade later, David Hieatt decided to do something about it.

Ironically, in 2009, David had found himself in a position similar to that of the unemployed jeans makers from the factory in Cardigan. In 1995 he had co-founded a successful clothing brand in London called Howies, which sold eco-friendly t-shirts, jeans and outdoor clothing, and in 2001 he re-located the company to Wales. After a rush of success the business became bigger than expected and larger than its staff could manage. With the intention of saving the business, Howies was sold to the large American brand Timberland in 2006, but with the fundamental proviso that the business remained in Wales. However, after eighteen months, 'market forces' took over and David found himself sitting in a meeting being told that the Howies warehouse was being moved to Holland and the design office was being moved to Denver – shortly thereafter, he left. Therefore, similar to the way in which the employees of the jeans factory in Cardigan had their livelihood taken away from them after they had invested their life and souls into making jeans, David also found himself in Cardigan and separated from the business and livelihood that he had built and loved.

After spending some time recovering from his loss, his love of jeans and his ability to recognise a lucky opportunity combined to create a spark of inspiration; David realised that he wanted to 'get Cardigan making jeans again'. When asked to describe his 'eureka' moment in an interview, David replied, 'It wasn't about starting another jeans brand. The world had enough of them. This jeans company was about getting a town that used to make jeans, to make them again. That was the "why" of it. It was all about the Town. And it is about bringing manufacturing back home'.[30]

Since my research into more sustainable and ethical ways of manufacturing garments, and doing business, began in Hong Kong over ten years ago, I have continued to search for projects that I believe are making a real difference. In doing so I have come across many businesses and individuals all over the world who are really trying to make a difference but many only manage it in a partial way. For instance, some small clothing brands use organic fabrics but they still manufacture in giant industrial factories overseas, and some niche businesses openly address ethical and environment issues here in Britain but still use traditional capitalist values to organise and run their project, which means they still end up controlling their employees rather than finding ways that allow them to genuinely thrive.

I read *Let My People Go Surfing* by the founder of the California-based outdoor clothing brand Patagonia whilst studying for a Masters degree in Corporate Environmental Governance in Hong Kong. On discovering Patagonia I felt as though I had uncovered a benchmark for business, one which expresses and consciously integrates a commitment to life into every single part of the whole business. In addition to respecting the planet and its people, in every way possible, and redesigning a business model to serve the life that sustained them (rather than existing to only serve, and be subordinate to, shareholders, of which they had none) Yvon Chouinard, the founder of Patagonia, literally *let his people go surfing*. When the surf was good the employees were allowed to leave their desks and take advantage of the local coastline that they loved. This was quite unlike anything I had ever heard of before, and had found since; that is until by chance, I had the good fortune to visit David Hieatt at the Hiut Denim factory in Cardigan, whilst holidaying with friends in Wales last summer.

The moment I entered Hiut's small factory I was blown away. I had never before experienced a clothing manufacturer quite like it, and out of all my time spent in the garment industry and in researching sustainability initiatives, I have never met a manager quite like David. Both the Hiut factory and David felt incredibly radical to me, yet in the most down-to-earth and pragmatic way.

The factory floor itself was full of life. As we stood in the sewing area and spoke with David, who was dressed very casually in jeans and a t-shirt, the radio was blaring out full blast in the background and the air was filled with the enticing aroma of good, strong coffee. Right in front of us were the sewing machines that Hiut use to create its small number of jeans (on a good day they make ten pairs). Even this sewing floor was quite unlike anything I had seen before, for a start, it was beautiful – each sewing machine was surrounded by a pine 'work station'. The walls were also clad in pitch pine, which is apparently from an old flour mill.[31] The aesthetic, and the feel, of this sewing area was warm and inviting. A short distance away, I could see the people making the jeans – they were laughing and smiling, full of life. This experience stood in stark contrast to the sterile, regimented factories I had visited in South-East Asia, which were usually painted in white or grey monotones, furnished minimally with cold metal and plastic, and flooded with strip lighting that only served to highlight the stark lack of humanity.

That is not to say that Hiut's sewing floor was fitted out in a decadent way, far from it. Everything had a purpose, but that purpose was delivered with genuine integrity, and a kind of passionate reverence for life, that seems to express itself (in everything Hiut Denim does) in a well-appointed yet unstated, quiet way. It is obvious that Hiut is not trying to impress. Their mission, and motto, is to 'do one thing well', and that one thing is jeans. In fact, Hiut make jeans so well that the people who make them sign their initials with pride on every single pair of jeans that they make. However, Hiut Denim doesn't just *do* that 'one thing well', what is equally important is that they only 'do' *one thing*. For instance, they say they will never branch out into hats, bags, or t-shirts, and will only ever make excellent, long lasting jeans. This means that Hiut's employees can focus their time and energy on doing *everything* well, whether it is the way in which they tell their story, the way that their manufacturing process impacts the environment, the respect and care given to the people who work for, or with the business, or the way that they design their sewing floor.

When visiting Hiut it wasn't just the factory and the product that blew me away. I was amazed by David's attitude to management and the way in which the business has been designed as whole. His approach is to employ experienced 'experts', or 'grand masters' as he calls them, and then let them get on with what they do best. David told me that the jeans makers don't have set hours, he gives them their workload and then lets them work to their own schedule. During our visit he said, 'They are adults, they can sort themselves out.' This was music to my ears, and a far cry from the approach to employment that I was confronted with in many South-East Asian factories.

The difference between the lively individuals that I encountered busily chatting and laughing as they worked at Hiut is almost incomprehensible in comparison to the people I observed making my designs in the huge industrial factories that I visited whilst working in Hong Kong. On reflection, I noticed that these contrasting ways of working form two very different approaches to life and to business – one in which life generally suffers and in the other life quite obviously thrives. I believe that this ability for life to thrive within a business is just as much down to the design and running of the business as a whole, as it is the honorable intention to do 'good things'. Through his lived experience in business David has stumbled upon what I think is a crucial dynamic, and understanding, that the other 'sustainable' or 'ethical' projects and businesses that I have encountered have missed. This dynamic and understanding is the way in which the 'whole' (or life) expresses itself in every part of the business. For example, David has recognised that to do 'one' thing well, *everything* must be done well, and that if the business is to thrive as whole, then the living parts of which it consists must thrive also. This is actively expressed in the way in which Hiut Denim gives so much trust, care, freedom and autonomy to its staff – and from what I could see, Hiut's employees certainly appeared to be thriving.

David seems to have an understanding of what it means for the life of a business to thrive 'from the inside'. He has a long, in-depth, lived experience of doing work that he loves and understands what it feels like to be enlivened by that work. During his time being employed by Timberland to run Howies, David also appears to have experienced the opposite: having that love, and vitality, eroded by a business model that values money more than it values life, including the life of the people that it employs. In his blog David wrote that people don't leave companies for money, he writes, 'They leave emotionally long before they leave physically. They leave because they are not valued, they are not being challenged or feel part of something that matters to them'.[32] What David thinks is central to this discontent is the failure of a business to keep its people continuously engaged in learning. In his book, *Do Purpose: Why Brands With a Purpose Do Better and Matter More*, David affirms:

> It's your job to create a learning culture that will keep them emotionally connected. You have to keep their hearts in the business. Training is the best way I know to do that. And it isn't just training to do their job better. That's standard stuff. But you will need to go beyond that to get people engaged. You will need to send them on courses, even if that course is unrelated to what they do with you. The best companies see the whole person, and not just the little segment that they do for you.[33]

Aside from treating their employees well Hiut does its best to treat the environment well too. The company does this by creating a product that fulfills a genuine human need (for clothing), by designing it to last, and through actively encouraging its customers to develop a relationship with the pair of jeans that they buy. This 'relationship' is actively nurtured so that Hiut's customers don't just 'use' their jeans and treat them as if they are highly disposable, instead they intentionally lead the customer to become emotionally engaged with their pair of jeans.

Current research shows that eighty percent of the environmental impact of jeans arises in the washing of them. In response to this Hiut started a 'No Wash club'. According to David and many other serious lovers of jeans, jeans look better when they remain unwashed. By signing up to the 'No Wash Club' the customers make a pact not to wash the jeans for six months – if they are successful at this David's says that it transforms the Hiut jeans into the 'greenest jean on the planet', potentially saving nearly a ton of carbon emissions and using 952 fewer litres of water.[34] As bizarre as this may sound, it is just indicative of the way in which Hiut addresses the global issues of our time, with novel, creative ideas, that can contribute to the resolution of systemic problems on a local level.

Another unique aspect of Hiut Denim is that they specialise in using 'raw' denim, which unlike the regular version, is not washed during the manufacturing process. This stops the indigo dye from running into the local water supply and saves larges amounts of water. Raw denim jeans have can have quite a severe look and feel initially as the material is stiff to begin with. Therefore, it takes time to soften and develop the 'worn in' look that is popular with customers. Most jean makers achieve this look industrially by washing the jeans many times and using harsh chemicals to artificially 'distress' them but Hiut are currently trialing a new environmentally friendly distressing method.

Instead of wasting water, and chemicals, Hiut is turning to people power to 'distress' their jeans, by employing fifty local people to be what they call, 'denim breakers'. Each one of these 'breakers' wears one pair of jeans over a six month period without washing them. The jeans are then given back to Hiut and expertly washed. These worn jeans, along with their new 'fashionably' distressed look, are then sold at a premium to those customers who want to bypass the six month wearing-in stage. Hiut is very open with the fact that this is an experiment, and that it might succeed, but also might fail. However, either way, what it does do is demonstrate the company's openness to trying something new. This creative experiment also reiterates the way in which Hiut's intention 'to do one thing well' is not just tied directly to their profit margins. For Hiut, doing one thing well means first and foremost 'doing well' by the planet and the people which make it possible for the company's income to flow in the first place.

What is also impressive is the way in which Hiut uses what some may consider to be their 'weaknesses' to their advantage. One of the 'weaknesses' is a near zero marketing budget, which David says is about the same size as their coffee budget. Size is another, making around ten pairs of jeans a day means that, in the grand scale of things,

Hiut jeans are a very tiny drop, in a very, very large ocean full of denim. However, the company has transformed these potential 'issues' into definite advantages. For example, as they are a small maker, Hiut can offer very unique services, such as a lifetime's free repairs and the offer of bespoke appointments via Facetime to create a unique, personalised pair of jeans. When I visited the Hiut factory David said that one of the main reasons that they were able to survive in global market was the way in which they had built the customer base for their business almost entirely on social media. By using these, mostly free, digital tools Hiut can reach and develop relationships with customers all over the world. During our visit David said that this process is time intensive but it is precisely what allows them to 'do' what they do.

This investment in time-consuming processes does not seem to present a problem to Hiut, the company has an inherently 'long-term' way of thinking and believes that good things should be given time to grow slowly. This value of 'slowness' is included in every part of their business as whole. For example, Hiut has recently launched a pair of jeans for women which took eighteen months to develop. In mainstream factories a product developer would be lucky to be given six months to develop one style, and nowadays many high-fashion garments are developed in a number of weeks, not months.

What is also particularly unusual, for a business, is that Hiut Denim have included a 'User Manual' on their website, which acts as a kind of 'roadmap' to show exactly how the company has come into being.[35] This includes interesting facts which shed further light on *how* Hiut have become who they currently are, such as the way in which, from the very start, Hiut intended to have no debt. Instead, to raise working capital, they approached a small number of shareholders 'who understand that it takes time to build something of value'[36], and in raising money by selling shares it means that the company have no business loans to repay. David seems to understand all too well the damaging effects that giving control away to shareholders can have and so Hiut has created two types of shares. One is a voting share, the other is a non-voting share, and the voting shares are not up for sale. This keeps control of the business well and truly in their own hands. Also, instead of giving their shareholders dividends, the business was designed to keep re-investing its profits, as Hiut believes that, 'The compound interest of investing back into the business will overtime be far greater than giving dividends to shareholders'.[37]

Hiut Denim have purpose, they have creative, innovative ideas, and they seem to understand that in order to truly do one thing well, *everything* must be done well. Through walking their talk, and putting this dynamic understanding into practice, Hiut is a living example of a business that not only helps to sustain those who are a part of it (staff and customers included), but which genuinely satisfies those people by creating the best possible conditions for their lives to thrive.

What each of these four projects, and their co-founders, demonstrate is that by giving our full attention to life, whether it is in the classrooms in which we teach; the residential estates where we live; the community centres in which we work; or the businesses that we build; we can get to know life in terms of itself, and we can allow this understanding of life to inform our own personal and professional growth and development. These projects also all display a radical form of honesty and openness, by openly sharing their experiences and explicitly communicating the details of the ways in which they 'do' what they do. In this way, each of these projects and organisations provide us with a kind of unconventional approach to open-source project design and development, offering us a starting point from which to create the best possible conditions for life to thrive in our own communities, schools, offices and businesses.

These projects, and the work of their co-founders, have also shown us the ways in which the world can come alive when we allow life to become its own theory and when we use this foundation of living knowledge to design our projects and businesses. The enthusiasm of the children participating in the 'Learning in Depth' initiative, who were leading their own inquiries at school, and the animated machinists at the Hiut Denim company, who were self-regulating their own work schedules in the factory, are beautiful examples of the ways in which parts of life can thrive when whole systems intentionally give their parts the freedom to do so.

Each of these projects demonstrates a way of being *whole*, which treats employees, students, and citizens as whole people; plants and animals as whole organisms; understands eco-systems as whole living systems; and most fundamentally, they each acknowledge that the planet is the biggest whole of all, and that it is the one which their existence is the most dependent upon.

In putting this dynamic understanding of wholeness into practice these projects reveal not just fragmented, partial solutions to sustainability but offer us ways of resolving global issues, such as poverty and unemployment, deteriorating natural and social environments, and failing educational systems and economies – at the root of the problem, on the ground and in a local context. As a result, each project in this chapter provides a beacon of hope for those looking to co-create a happier, healthier, and more peaceful, sustainable world.

Conclusion: From Surviving to Thriving

In times of universal deceit, telling the truth becomes a revolutionary act.

George Orwell

An end is only a new beginning...

At the root of everything we create is the mind that created it, including the organisations in which we work and the societies in which we live. This is why a dynamic way of seeing is so important in relation to the current state of the world today. Its capacity to get to know life *as it is* liberates both us and the world from the limiting habits of our everyday perception; from the partial knowledge that the left-hemisphere of our brain constructs; and from the collective blind-spots that converge to form 'business as usual'.

For as long as a person, or a group of people, remains unaware of the ways in which the human mind defines and limits our experience of the world, then their own potential to know, to act, to innovate and to interact will be limited. However, once these limitations have appeared within our awareness, we become free to notice life *as it is*, and to develop a dynamic way of seeing that is flexible, adaptable and responsive to life.

This dynamic way of seeing shines a light on the conditions within which life is most likely to flourish and therefore makes it possible for us to replicate these conditions. If we wish to thrive as individuals, we must position this light on our own lives *and* on the lives of the people, the places and the parts of nature that we interact with. We cannot thrive on our own because absolute independence does not exist, it is a construct of our mind and is not true to life itself. Whilst we are busy being 'independent' in the world, or cutting ourselves off from mainstream life in order to be 'self-sufficient', the rest of the 7.2 billion parts of our collective human body continue to significantly, and often negatively, impact the life and living eco-systems that we rely on to sustain our selves. Consequently, figuring out how we can thrive as individuals, necessarily requires us to develop an understanding of life in context, just like the work of Craig Holdrege at The Nature Institute.

In his work on Human Scale Development, Manfred Max-Neef wrote that for Latin America to develop a healthy, self-sustaining economy its efforts must be focused on the genuine and synergistic satisfaction of human needs. He believes that this is possible through the development of small, organic ventures that are in a position to respond flexibly to the complex and unique conditions of the life that surrounds them. This way of creating a healthy, self-sustaining economy (and community) is equally valid for all parts of the world and the Welsh denim brand Hiut provides a clear example of what these small, organic ventures can look like and how they can be created.

By learning to discern which projects, organisations or businesses *are* actively creating the conditions that are needed for life to thrive, such as the research projects we explored in Chapter 7 and the case studies from Chapter 8, we can consciously choose to learn from, and interact with, these types of project in order to satisfy our own needs. This is how we can individually contribute towards enlivening, not just our whole selves, but also the larger 'wholes' of which we are a part. In doing so, we enter into a self-perpetuating cycle of enlivenment and satisfaction.

If every part of our whole 7.2 billion human body decided to follow Hiut's example of doing 'one' thing (and every part of it) well, in their personal *and* professional lives, we could create a world in which both humans and nature could flourish and thrive. Or as the author Charles Eisenstein puts it, we could create 'the more beautiful world that our hearts know is possible'.

In terms of our everyday lives, living attentively may well be the end of our world as we know it, or as we *thought* we knew it, and this can be extremely difficult to come to terms with, but every ending is also a new beginning. In order to give life a chance, or to give ourselves a chance to really see life as it is, we need to constantly be prepared to let go of what we think we already know. The more adept we become at letting go, and at opening ourselves to the unknown, the freer we then become to allow new life, new circumstances, new people, and new discoveries into our everyday lives, workplaces, and societies. 'Everything we already know is worth being a bit suspicious of. To genuinely not know creates a space for the unknown to become known in terms of itself. It is out of the open space of not knowing, that knowing arises'.[1]

Just as we can never step in the 'same' river twice, we can never read the 'same' book twice, for even in the time in-between starting and finishing a book we have already changed, or evolved, in some way. Life has already moved on from where it was when we read that first page. Each time we interact with a part of life both us, and life, have changed, whether we are aware of it or not. Therefore, I urge you to let go of what you think you know and to return to the beginning of *First Steps to Seeing*. Let it continue to guide you towards seeing the world anew, as if for the first time, even if it is for the thousandth time. As T.S. Eliot wrote: 'We shall not cease from exploration, and the end of all our exploring will be to arrive where we started and know the place for the first time.'

In a similar way to the Zen monks who have achieved enlightenment, we must return again to chop wood and carry water. The difference will not necessarily be in our everyday tasks, or in the work that we choose to do, but in the awareness that we bring to the enactment of each task; as the key to living attentively, and to developing a dynamic way of seeing, is not *what* we do but *the way in which* we do it.

Endnotes

Introduction

1. Frederick Franck, *The Zen of Seeing: Seeing/Drawing as Meditation*, London: Wildwood House (1976), p. 113.
2. John Medina, *Brain Rules*, Seattle, WA: Pear Press (2014), p. 124.

Chapter 1

1. John Medina, *Brain Rules*, Seattle, WA: Pear Press (2014), p. 184.
2. Iain McGilchrist, *The Master and his Emissary: The Divided Brain and the Making of the Western World*, New Haven: Yale University Press (2010), p. 38.
3. *Ibid.* p. 31.
4. See for example Henri Bortoft, 'The Organizing Idea in Cognitive Perception', in *The Wholeness of Nature: Goethe's Way of Science*, Edinburgh: Floris Books (1996), p. 123.
5. *Ibid.* p. 125.
6. *Ibid.* p. 131.
7. I was first introduced to the Face/Vase drawing exercise at the Norwich School of Art eighteen years ago. See Betty Edwards, 'Crossing Over: Experiencing the Shift From Left to Right', *Drawing on the Right Hand Side of the Brain*, London: Harper Collins (1993), p. 45.
8. Iain McGilchrist, *The Master and his Emissary: The Divided Brain and the Making of the Western World*, New Haven: Yale University Press (2010), p. 27.
9. *Ibid.* p. 31.
10. Mary Oliver, *Long Life: Essays and Other Writings*, Boston, MA: Da Capo Press (2004), p. 91.

Chapter 2

1. James Hillman, *The Thought of the Heart and the Soul of the World*, Putnam, CT: Spring Publications (1992), p. 115.
2. See for example John Shotter 'Understanding Process From Within: An Argument for 'Withness'- Thinking', *Organization Studies*, Vol. 27, No. 4, (2006) p. 585.

3. Daniel Kahneman, *Thinking, Fast and Slow*, London: Penguin Books (2012), p. 393.
4. *Ibid.* pp. 394-95.
5. John Medina, *Brain Rules*, Seattle, WA: Pear Press (2014), p. 115.
6. *Ibid.* p. 120.
7. Henri Bortoft, *Taking Appearance Seriously: The Dynamic Way of Seeing in Goethe and European Thought*, Edinburgh: Floris Books (2012), p. 17.
8. James Hillman, *The Thought of the Heart and the Soul of the World,* Putnam, CT: Spring Publications (1992), p. 115.
9. *Ibid.* p. 115–116.
10. Jack L. Seymour, Margaret A. Crain, and Joseph V. Crockett, *Educating Christians*, Nashville, TN: Abingdon Press (1993), p. 53.
11. I was first introduced to 'exact sense perception' by teachers at Schumacher College in Devon, such as Craig Holdrege, Terry Irwin, Philip Franses and Stephan Harding. The technique was taught within the context of practising 'Goethean Science', a phenomenological inquiry into the life of nature.
12. Hans-Georg Gadamer, *Truth and Method*, New York: Harper and Row (1962), p. 58, cited by Henri Bortoft, 'Counterfeit and Authentic Wholes: Finding a Means for Dwelling in Nature' in *Goethe's Way of Science: A Phenomenology of Nature*, eds. David Seamon and Arthur Zajonc, Albany, NY: State University of New York Press (1998), p. 295.
13. Henri Bortoft 'The Whole: Counterfeit and Authentic', *Systematics*, Vol. 9, No. 2, (1971) p. 24.
14. Frederick Franck, *The Zen of Seeing: Seeing/Drawing as Meditation*, London: Wildwood House (1976), p. 8.
15. Henri Bortoft, Schumacher College lectures, (Audio recording 0027), September 2012.
16. Emma Kidd *Re-cognition: The Re-cognition of our Connection to Nature Through Goethe's Way of Seeing*, Schumacher College, Totnes, (2009) p. 75. This dissertation can be downloaded from the blog *Transition Consciousness* (www.transitionconsciousness.org) here: http://wp.me/p11Bag-mX.
17. Henri Bortoft, *The Wholeness of Nature: Goethe's Way of Science*, Edinburgh: Floris Books (1996), p. 66.
18. Todd Kashdan, *Curious?: Discover the Missing Ingredient to a Fulfilling Life*, New York: Harper Collins (2009), p. 57.
19. See for example Judy Willis 'Brain-Based Teaching Strategies for Improving Students' Memory, Learning, and Test-Taking Success', *Childhood Education*, Vol. 83, No. 5, (2007) p. 310.

Chapter 3

1. Craig Holdrege, *Thinking Like a Plant: A Living Science for Life*, Great Barrington, MA: Lindisfarne Books (2013), p. 57.
2. Arthur Zajonc, *Meditation as Contemplative Inquiry: When Knowing Becomes Love*, Great Barrington, MA: Lindisfarne Books (2009), p. 71.

3. John Medina, *Brain Rules*, Seattle, WA: Pear Press (2014), p. 95.
4. Henri Bortoft, Schumacher College lectures (Audio recording 0026), September 2012.
5. Nigel Hoffmann, *Goethe's Science of Living Form: The Artistic Stages*, Hillsdale, NY: Adonis Press (2007), p. 38.
6. Henri Bortoft, *The Wholeness of Nature: Goethe's Way of Science*, Edinburgh: Floris Books (1996), p. 40.
7. See for example Henri Bortoft, *The Wholeness of Nature: Goethe's Way of Science*, Edinburgh: Floris Books (1996), p. 191.
8. Pat Williams 'Casting New Light', *Human Givens*, Vol. 8, No. 4, (2001) p. 25.
9. If you would like to repeat Goethe's prism experiments yourself and to further understand their relationship to Newton's work then I highly recommend Henri Bortoft's description of the experiments in *The Wholeness of Nature: Goethe's Way of Science*, Edinburgh: Floris Books (1996), p. 40.
10. *Ibid.* p. 43.
11. Henri Bortoft, 'The Transformative Potential of Paradox', *Holistic Science Journal*, Vol. 1, No. 1, (2010) p. 33.
12. Arthur Zajonc, *Meditation as Contemplative Inquiry: When Knowing Becomes Love*, Great Barrington, MA: Lindisfarne Books (2009), p. 84.

Chapter 4

1. Henri Cartier-Bresson, *The Mind's Eye: Writings on Photography and Photographers*, New York: Aperture (1999), pp. 15ff, cited by Howard Zehr, *The Little Book of Contemplative Photography: Seeing with Wonder, Respect and Humility*, Intercourse, PA: Good Books (2005), p. 2.
2. Howard Zehr, *The Little Book of Contemplative Photography: Seeing with Wonder, Respect and Humility*, Intercourse, PA: Good Books (2005), p. 65.
3. Nigel Hoffmann, *Goethe's Science of Living Form: The Artistic Stages*, Hillsdale, NY: Adonis Press (2007), p. 44.
4. Arthur Zajonc, *Meditation as Contemplative Inquiry: When Knowing Becomes Love*, Great Barrington, MA: Lindisfarne Books (2009), p. 39.
5. Henri Bortoft 'The Whole: Counterfeit and Authentic', *Systematics*, Vol. 9, No. 2, (1971) p. 11.
6. Henri Bortoft, *The Wholeness of Nature: Goethe's Way of Science*, Edinburgh: Floris Books (1996), p. 4.
7. I have adapted Henri Bortoft's metaphor of using a hologram, and holographic plate, to describe the nature of wholeness by adding an iconic movie character as the subject of our hologram, in order to assist our understanding and to further enliven the organising idea of an authentic whole.
8. Henri Bortoft 'The Whole: Counterfeit and Authentic', *Systematics*, Vol. 9, No. 2, (1971) p. 7.
9. Emma Kidd *Re-cognition: The Re-cognition of our Connection to Nature Through Goethe's Way of Seeing*, Schumacher College, Totnes, (2009) p. 75.

This dissertation can be downloaded from the blog *Transition Consciousness* (www.transitionconsciousness.org) here: http://wp.me/p11Bag-mX.

Chapter 5

1. Frederick Franck, *The Zen of Seeing: Seeing/Drawing as Meditation*, London: Wildwood House (1976), p. 121.
2. *Ibid.* pp. 26–27.
3. Todd Kashdan, *Curious?: Discover the Missing Ingredient to a Fulfilling Life*, New York: Harper Collins (2009), p. 38.
4. Ester Perel, *Mating In Captivity: Sex, Lies and Domestic Bliss*, London: Hodder and Stoughton (2007), p. 25.
5. Todd Kashdan, *Curious?: Discover the Missing Ingredient to a Fulfilling Life*, New York: Harper Collins (2009), p. 35.
6. John Medina, *Brain Rules*, Seattle, WA: Pear Press (2014), p. 252.
7. Todd Kashdan, *Curious?: Discover the Missing Ingredient to a Fulfilling Life*, New York: Harper Collins (2009), p. 17.
8. Brian Goodwin, *Nature's Due: Healing Our Fragmented Culture*, Edinburgh: Floris Books (2007), pp. 156-57.
9. Arthur Zajonc 'Cognitive-Affective Connections in Teaching and Learning: The Relationship Between Love and Knowledge', *Journal of Cognitive Affective Learning*, Vol. 3, No. 1, (2006) p. 8.
10. *Ibid.* p. 1.

Chapter 6

1. Brené Brown, *The Gifts of Imperfection: Let Go of Who You Think You're Supposed to Be and Embrace Who You Are*, Minneapolis, MN: Hazelden (2010), p. 6.
2. Todd Kashdan, *Curious?: Discover the Missing Ingredient to a Fulfilling Life*, New York: Harper Collins (2009), p. 27.
3. Brené Brown, *Daring Greatly: How the Courage to Be Vulnerable Transforms the Way We Live, Love, Parent and Lead*, New York: Gotham (2012), p. 37.
4. Augusten Burroughs, *This Is How: Surviving What You Think You Can't*, New York: Picador (2012), p. 26.
5. See for example the audio recording by Pema Chödrön, 'The Propensity to Be Bothered', *When Pain Is the Doorway: Awakening in the Most Difficult Circumstances*, Louisville, CO: Sounds True (2013).
6. Quote by Pema Chödrön in 'Women's Wisdom, Part 3: Pema Chödrön's Birthday Wish – Practising Peace', *The Huffington Post*, June 18, (2013), www.huffingtonpost.com/ michaela-haas/womens-wisdom-part-3-pe-ma_b_3424338. html.
7. Pema Chödrön, The Omega Institute lectures, Rhinebeck, NY, 'Basic Goodness', September 26-28, (2014).

8. Stephen Jenkinson quoted in article by Ian Mackenzie, 'Stephen Jenkinson on the Meaning of Death', August 07, (2013), http://www.dailygood.org/2013/08/07/stephen-jenkinson-on-the-meaning-of-death/.
9. Todd Kashdan, *Curious?: Discover the Missing Ingredient to a Fulfilling Life*, New York: Harper Collins (2009), p. 34.

Chapter 7

1. Adyashanti, *Falling Into Grace: Insights on the End of Suffering*, Boulder, CO: Sounds True (2013), pp. 229-30.
2. Todd Kashdan, *Curious?: Discover the Missing Ingredient to a Fulfilling Life*, New York: Harper Collins (2009), p. 26.
3. The term 'bracketing' refers to the first stage in the process of phenomenological inquiry which involves both getting knowing and setting aside our assumptions. 'When we enter into the phenomenological attitude, we suspend our beliefs, and we bracket the world and all the things in the world ... When we so bracket the world or some particular object, we do not turn it into a mere appearance, an illusion, a mere idea, or any other sort of merely subjective impression. Rather, we now consider it precisely as it is intended by an intentionality in the natural attitude.' Robert Sokolowski, *Introduction to Phenomenology*, Cambridge: Cambridge University Press (2000), p. 49.
4. John Gottman and Nan Silver, *The Seven Principles For Making Marriage Work*, London: Orion (2007), p. 1.
5. *Ibid.* pp. 27–34.
6. Douglas Stone, Bruce Patton and Sheila Heen, *Difficult Conversations: How to Discuss What Matters Most*, New York: Portfolio Penguin (2011), p. 7.
7. *Ibid.* p. 39.
8. *Ibid.* p. 40.
9. *Ibid.* p. 59.
10. *Ibid.* p. 59.
11. See http://www.why-me.org/.
12. Daniel Goleman, *Focus: The Hidden Driver of Excellence*, New York: Harper (2013), p. 74.

Chapter 8

1. Quoted from the cover of the Hiut Denim Company Yearbook, No. 2, 2014.

CASE STUDY: HUMAN SCALE DEVELOPMENT

2. Colin Tudge, *Economic Renaissance: Holistic Economics for the 21st Century*, Totnes: Green Books (2008), p. 11.

3. See for example Gerhard Drekonja-Kornat 'El desarrollo a la medida humana', *D+C Desarrollo y Cooperación*, No. 2, (2002) pp. 25-29, accessed at http://www.max-neef.cl/.

4. 'Chilean Economist Manfred Max-Neef: US Is Becoming an "Underdeveloping Nation"', *Democracy Now*, September 22, 2010, http://www.democracynow.org/ 2010/9/22/chilean_economist_manfred_max_neef_us.

5. Manfred Max-Neef, *Human Scale Development*, New York and London: Apex Press (1991), p. 16ff, cited by Philip B Smith and Manfred Max-Neef, *Economics Unmasked: From Power and Greed to Compassion and the Common Good*, Totnes: Green Books (2011), p. 141.

6. Manfred Max-Neef, *Human Scale Development*, New York and London: Apex Press (1991), p. vii.

7. Philip B. Smith and Manfred Max-Neef, *Economics Unmasked: From Power and Greed to Compassion and the Common Good*, Totnes: Green Books (2011), p. 176.

8. Paul Ekins & Manfred Max-Neef, *Real-Life Economics: Understanding Wealth Creation*, London: Routledge (1992), p. 200.

9. Philip B. Smith & Manfred Max-Neef, *Economics Unmasked: From Power and Greed to Compassion and the Common Good*, Totnes: Green Books, (2011), p. 17.

10. 'Chilean Economist Manfred Max-Neef: US Is Becoming an "Underdeveloping Nation"', *Democracy Now*, September 22, 2010, http://www.democracynow.org/ 2010/9/22/chilean_economist_manfred_max_neef_us.

CASE STUDY: LEARNING IN DEPTH

11. Kieran Egan, *The Educated Mind: How Cognitive Tools Shape Our Understanding*, Chicago and London: The University of Chicago Press (1997), p. 1.

12. *Ibid*. p. 10.

13. *Ibid*. p. 172.

14. Kieran Egan, *Getting It Wrong From The Beginning: Our Progressivist Inheritance from Herbert Spencer, John Dewey, and Jean Piaget*, New Haven and London: Yale University Press, (2002), p. 62.

15. *Ibid*. p. 63.

16. See http://www.ierg.ca.

17. Kieran Egan, *Learning In Depth: A Simple Innovation That Can Transform Schooling*, Chicago and London: The University of Chicago Press (2010), p. 213.

18. See http://ierg.ca/news/news-archive-2006-2012/.

19. See http://www.ierg.net/LiD/.

20. Excerpt from a letter written by a parent of child participating in the LiD initiative. See http://ierg.ca/LID/.

21. See http://ierg.ca/LID/.

22. Kieran Egan, *Learning In Depth: A Simple Innovation That Can Transform Schooling*, Chicago and London: The University of Chicago Press (2010), p. 187.

CASE STUDY: THE NATURE INSTITUTE

23. See http://natureinstitute.org/about/staff/choldrege.htm.
24. Craig Holdrege 'What Does It Mean to Be a Sloth?' *The Nature Institute* (2009) http://natureinstitute.org/nature/sloth.htm. This is a revised version of an article originally written by Craig Holdrege, published in the *Newsletter of the Society for the Evolution of Science*, Vol. 14, No. 1, (1998) pp. 1–26.
25. See http://natureinstitute.org/nature/sloth.htm.
26. Craig Holdrege, Schumacher College lectures, September 19, (2008).
27. Craig Holdrege, *A Question of Genes: Understanding Life in Context*, Edinburgh: Floris Books (1996), p. 124.
28. See http://natureinstitute.org/nontarget/.
29. Craig Holdrege, *Thinking Like a Plant: A Living Science for Life*, Great Barrington, MA: Lindisfarne Books (2013), p. 187.

CASE STUDY: HIUT DENIM

30. 'Interview with David Hieatt Owner and Founder of Hiut Denim', *OEN*, March 02, 2012, http://the189.com/feature/interview-with-david-hieatt-owner-and-founder-of-hiut-denim/.
31. 'Hiut Denim Co: The jeans with the app that tells their history', *The Telegraph,* March 23, 2012, http://fashion.telegraph.co.uk/article/TMG9161337/Hiut-Denim-Co-The-jeans-with-the-app-that-tells-their-history.html.
32. David Hieatt, 'Most People Leave Companies Via The Window', September 25, (2014), http://davidhieatt.typepad.com/doonethingwell/2014/09/most-people-leave-companies-via-the-window.html.
33. David Hieatt, *Do Purpose: Why Brands With a Purpose Do Better and Matter More*, London: The Do Book Company, (2014), p. 127.
34. 'Day 2 – David Hieatt, Hiut Denim', June 16, (2014), https://www.youtube.com/watch?v=ivsfiQvvR38
35. See http://hiutdenim.co.uk/blogs/story/4801552-our-user-manual.
36. See point number three, 'A Small Number of Shareholders.', http://hiutdenim.co.uk/blogs/story/4801552-our-user-manual.
37. See point number sixteen, 'We won't pay a dividend. We will keep re-investing.', http://hiutdenim.co.uk/blogs/story/4801552-our-user-manual.

Conclusion

1. Notes from a Phenomenology Masterclass hosted by No-where consultancy group, London, July (2012).

Bibliography

Adyashanti (2013) *Falling Into Grace: Insights on the End of Suffering*, Sounds True, Boulder.

Bortoft, Henri (1996) *The Wholeness of Nature: Goethe's Way of Science*, Floris Books, Edinburgh.

—, (2012) *Taking Appearance Seriously: The Dynamic Way of Seeing in Goethe and European Thought*, Floris Books, Edinburgh.

Brown, Brené (2010) *The Gifts of Imperfection: Let Go of Who You Think You're Supposed to Be and Embrace Who You Are*, Hazelden, Minneapolis.

—, (2012) *Daring Greatly: How the Courage to Be Vulnerable Transforms the Way We Live, Love, Parent and Lead*, Gotham, New York.

Burroughs, Augusten (2012) *This Is How: Surviving What You Think You Can't*, Picador, New York.

Cartier-Bresson, Henri (1999) *The Mind's Eye: Writings on Photography and Photographers*, Aperture, New York.

Chouinard, Yvon (2006) *Let My People Go Surfing: The Education of a Reluctant Businessman*, Penguin Books, New York.

Edwards, Betty (1993) *Drawing on the Right Hand Side of the Brain*, Harper Collins, London.

Egan, Kieran (1997) *The Educated Mind: How Cognitive Tools Shape Our Understanding*, The University of Chicago Press, Chicago.

—, (2002) *Getting It Wrong From The Beginning: Our Progressivist Inheritance from Herbert Spencer, John Dewey, and Jean Piaget*, Yale University Press, New Haven.

—, (2010) *Learning In Depth: A Simple Innovation That Can Transform Schooling*, The University of Chicago Press, Chicago.

Ekins, Paul & Max-Neef, Manfred (1992) *Real-Life Economics: Understanding Wealth Creation*, Routledge, London.

Franck, Frederick (1976) *The Zen of Seeing: Seeing/Drawing as Meditation*, Wildwood House, London.

Gadamer, Hans-Georg (1962) *Truth and Method,* Harper and Row, New York.

Goodwin, Brian (2007) *Nature's Due: Healing Our Fragmented Culture*, Floris Books, Edinburgh.

Goleman, Daniel (2013) *Focus: The Hidden Driver of Excellence*, Harper, New York.

Gottman, John & Silver, Nan (2007) *The Seven Principles For Making Marriage Work*, Orion, London.

Hieatt, David (2014) *Do Purpose: Why Brands With a Purpose Do Better and Matter More*, The Do Book Company, London.

Hillman, James (1992) *The Thought of the Heart and the Soul of the World,* Spring Publications, Putnam.

Hoffmann, Nigel (2007) *Goethe's Science of Living Form: The Artistic Stages*, Adonis Press, Hillsdale.

Holdrege, Craig (1996) *A Question of Genes: Understanding Life in Context*, Floris Books, Edinburgh.

—, & Talbott, Steve (2008) *Beyond Biotechnology: The Barren Promise of Genetic Engineering,* The University Press of Kentucky, Lexington.

—, (2013) *Thinking Like a Plant: A Living Science for Life*, Lindisfarne Books, Great Barrington.

Kahneman, Daniel (2012) *Thinking, Fast and Slow*, Penguin Books, London.

Kashdan, Todd (2009) *Curious?: Discover the Missing Ingredient to a Fulfilling Life*, Harper Collins, New York.

Max-Neef, Manfred (1991) *Human Scale Development*, Apex Press, New York.

Medina, John (2014) *Brain Rules*, Pear Press, Seattle.

McGilchrist, Iain (2010) *The Master and his Emissary: The Divided Brain and the Making of the Western World*, Yale University Press, New Haven.

Oliver, Mary (2004) *Long Life: Essays and Other Writings,* Da Capo Press, Boston.

Perel, Ester (2007) *Mating In Captivity: Sex, Lies and Domestic Bliss*, Hodder and Stoughton, London.

Reason, Peter & Newman, Melanie (2013) *Stories of the Great Turning*, Vala Publishing Co-operative, Bristol.

Seamon, David & Zajonc, Arthur (1998) *Goethe's Way of Science: A Phenomenology of Nature*, State University of New York Press, Albany.

Seymour, Jack L., Crain, Margaret A., & Crockett, Joseph V. (1993) *Educating Christians*, Abingdon Press, Nashville.

Smith, Philip B. & Max-Neef, Manfred (2011) *Economics Unmasked: From Power and Greed to Compassion and the Common Good*, Green Books, Totnes.

Sokolowski, Robert (2000) *Introduction to Phenomenology*, Cambridge University Press, Cambridge.

Stone, Douglas, Patton, Bruce & Heen, Sheila (2011) *Difficult Conversations: How to Discuss What Matters Most*, Portfolio Penguin, New York.

Tudge, Colin (2008) *Economic Renaissance: Holistic Economics for the 21st Century*, Green Books, Totnes.

Zajonc, Arthur (2009) *Meditation as Contemplative Inquiry: When Knowing Becomes Love*, Lindisfarne Books, Great Barrington.

Zehr, Howard (2005) *The Little Book of Contemplative Photography: Seeing with Wonder, Respect and Humility*, Good Books, Intercourse.

Index

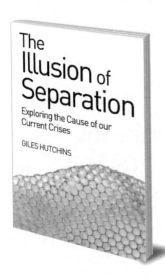

The Illusion of Separation
Exploring the Cause of our Current Crises

Giles Hutchins

Our modern patterns of thinking and learning are all based on observing a world of 'things', which we think of as separate building blocks. This worldview allows us to count and measure objects without their having any innate value; it provides neat definitions and a sense of control over life. However, this approach also sets humans apart from each other, and from nature.

In reality, in nature, everything is connected in a fluid, dynamic way. 'Separateness' is an illusion we have created – and is fast becoming a dangerous delusion infecting how we relate to business, politics, and other key areas of our daily reality.

Giles Hutchins argues that the source of our current social, economic and environmental issues springs from the misguided way we see and construct our world. With its roots in ancient wisdom, this insightful book sets out an accesssible, easy to follow exploration of the causes of our current crises, offering ways to rectify these issues at source and then pointing to a way ahead.

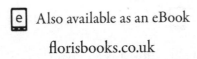

Also available as an eBook

florisbooks.co.uk

Taking Appearance Seriously

The Dynamic Way of Seeing in Goethe and European Thought

Henri Bortoft

The history of western metaphysics from Plato onwards is dominated by the dualism of being and appearance. What something really is (its true being) is believed to be hidden behind the 'mere appearances' through which it manifests. Twentieth-century European thinkers radically overturned this way of thinking. 'Appearance' began to be taken seriously, with the observer participating in the dynamic event of perception.

In this important book, Henri Bortoft guides us through this dynamic way of seeing, exploring issues including how we distinguish things, how we find meaning, and the relationship between thought and words.

Expanding the scope of his previous book, *The Wholeness of Nature*, Bortoft shows how Goethean insights combine with this dynamic way of seeing in continental philosophy, to offer an actively experienced 'life of meaning'.

This book will be of interest to anyone who wants to understand the contribution and wider implications of modern European thought in the world today.

 Also available as an eBook

florisbooks.co.uk